NATIONAL CROSS WALK

An Amazing Journey of Faith, Love and Endurance

Stephanie Guion Greiner

with Calvin Greiner

Partnership
Publications

Partnership Publications

www.h2hp.com

National Cross Walk:
An Amazing Journey of Faith, Love and Endurance
by Stephanie Guion Greiner with Calvin Greiner

© 2014 by Stephanie Guion Greiner with Calvin Greiner

Published by
Partnership Publications
A Division of House Publications
11 Toll Gate Road, Litiz, PA, USA
Tele: 717.627.1996

www.h2hp.com

ISBN-10: 0983156042
ISBN-13: 978-0-9831560-4-8

Printed in the United States of America

Dedication

To Henrietta Bailey Guion, my paternal grandmother,
an aspiring writer whose life was cut short—
you birthed our family's love of writing.

To Ed Guion, my dad—you taught me the power of
humor and a love of learning that shaped my life.

To Nielsen, our oldest son—you write from the heart;
you are braver than you know.

To Cassandra Arielle, our oldest granddaughter—
you have a writer's heart; through you the legacy continues.

To our five children, who are amazing,
incredible people—you make this Mama proud.

To our eight wonderful grandchildren—you give me
hope for the future and you keep this Grandma young.

To Calvin, my partner in life—
your faith, love and endurance inspire me every day.

In Loving Memory

Naomi "Grammy" Greiner

November 15, 1916 ~ August 22, 2014

Anker Nielsen, Jr.

July 31, 1917 ~ June 19, 2014

Contents

A Special Note to the Reader

Calvin and I began our cross-country prayer walk in February 2014 and completed it in August 2014. But those dates are merely a glimpse into the year-long season that encapsulated our epic adventure. We would like to paint a picture for you of how we received the vision for our walk, the season of preparation, and our daily experiences as we walked across the nation.

Our year-long adventure is interspersed with some short vignettes describing what we call "God Stories"—supernatural interventions and answers to prayer—that we experienced throughout our National Cross Walk experience. These impressions, recollections and musings are all part of our experience of living through an adventure of tremendous magnitude. Interspersed throughout the dialogue you will find historic facts, cultural insights, personal struggles and victories, and true accounts told through our eyes. Occasionally the names of people and places were changed or abbreviated to protect the privacy and integrity of sensitive information.

You may have noticed that the book is authored by me, with anecdotal contributions from my husband. I write in singular first-person for ease of writing and have attempted to relate as accurately as possible what both of us individually experienced—Calvin as the walker and me as his sole support person. Our experiences were unique and intimate.

The journal entries in the following pages were originally sent as email updates to our supporters and those following us as we journeyed cross country. Many people related to us that they felt as if they were able to envision and live the journey with us as they connected with us through these updates. Although these updates were certainly informational and helped paint a picture for our friends and family of what we were experiencing, they also served a much deeper purpose—that of helping me to process all the changes and challenges that I faced throughout the year long experience.

Our experience is documented in the film, "National Cross Walk 2014: An Amazing Journey of Faith, Love and Endurance," and is available upon request. May this book encourage, challenge and stir your hearts to live with abandon, fulfilling the special call that God has for each one of you.

Finding Joy on the Journey,

Stephanie Guion Greiner (October, 2014)

Introduction

"I'm not getting out of this bed until I have a breakthrough!"

My husband's words hung heavily in the air as I stood helplessly beside the bed, watching the dull January sun drop apathetically towards the horizon. His words could mean only two things: Either the Lord would come through for Calvin in a powerful way and raise him up from his past two and one-half months of depression and fatigue, or this nightmare of oppression would continue. Ever since we had made the decision to accept this assignment from the Lord—to prayer walk across the entire nation—we faced one obstacle after another. But Calvin's despair was the biggest test of all.

These episodes had come and gone before, but never of this magnitude and for this long of a season. My patience and energy were wearing thin. Did all the confirmations we felt that God had given us mean nothing? I felt sure my husband and I were being called—even compelled to journey into the wilderness of our nation's spiritual wasteland. Our purpose was to implore the God of Heaven to pour out His winds of revival once more upon our great land.

Calvin and I seemed to breeze through the preliminary preparations—meeting with a fellow prayer walker, submitting the vision to spiritual leaders we trusted, sharing our vision with our family, creating a brochure and business card and even laying the groundwork for our website. But when we started to visit churches and gatherings to share our vision and raise support, a weight of heaviness began to come over Calvin, and even every-day tasks became almost impossible for him.

As Calvin spent more and more hours in bed, wrestling with overwhelming thoughts of doubt and fear, completely devoid of the ability to concentrate and lacking physical strength, I began to take on the planning single-handedly as well as continue with my massage therapy work and run the household.

On work days, Calvin somehow pulled himself to life and dragged through his day, only to collapse into bed again upon his arrival home. Nights were filled with sleeplessness and anxiety. We were feeling increasingly desperate trying to figure out what was going on. We asked other believers we trusted to come and pray over him. In addition to praying, they also incorporated Theophostic Prayer Ministry, which focuses on identifying the lie-based core belief that we harbor and seeking the Lord in prayer to receive counsel through the presence of the Holy Spirit. Calvin and I also sought counsel from medical doctors and counselors. What had begun as a beautiful vision of love and sacrifice—traversing our great nation, praying for her survival, became a mocking irony. Now we were the ones trying to survive, grasping for hope.

It was two weeks before our launch: The last church had been visited, the route was planned, the hotels had been chosen, and we were beginning to pack our bags. I needed to start book-ing hotel reservations, but how could I go forward with our plans when Calvin's physical stamina had hit an all-time low, his body unconditioned from months of lying around?

The original plan had been for him to begin physical conditioning in October and work up to walking twenty miles a day, an average daily distance that we decided would be a reasonable goal for a prayer walk of this magnitude. Calvin had completed many prayer walks during the past thirty years. Each walk had been unique, but nothing like this one, where his mental, spiritual and physical reserves would be tested to the limit. The longest walk Calvin previously completed was his walk across the state of Pennsylvania in 2006 when he averaged 25 miles a day. That walk was only eleven days long and began in Lancaster County on September 11. Amazingly, the hotel room number, where he stayed in Pittsburgh was Room 911, which we felt confirmed the timing of the walk and brought glory to God. This particular walk was fraught with open, painful blisters on his feet and tired achy muscles. Now we were embarking on a six-month prayer walk, crossing 2,500 miles of difficult surfaces, exposed to all kinds of weather conditions, sleeping in different hotels, drinking strange water and battling unseen spiritual forces. How could we even consider the possibility that in two short weeks we would be driving to our starting point in West Liberty, West Virginia? Even the short six-hour drive in his condition would be unrealistic.

Ironically, the decision to walk across America was in some ways birthed through me, a reluctant and unlikely companion to many of Calvin's previous walks. The idea had started as I sat at the table helping with a bulk mailing at our church. Calvin had recently completed a successful prayer walk from Baltimore to Harrisburg in July 2013, which is probably why the conversation turned to Calvin's prayer walks and light discussion about where he had been and what he had accomplished. I never like being the object of attention in such settings, so I dove into the work at hand, hoping to redirect the conversation. And then the bomb was dropped—unexpectedly, unapologetically—it flew my way, taking me by surprise. "Has he ever considered doing a cross country prayer walk?" an intercessor posed innocently. Like Sarah, I chuckled at the absurdity of such a thought, the impossibility of such a feat.

"How would that be possible? It can't be done." My excuses began in earnest now, with me trying to convince myself that God would never call a man of 62 years to such an exploit. But the question hung like a veil before my eyes as I drove home that day. It was all I thought about; all I could focus on.

My husband's response was the same as mine when I posed the question to him later that day. "Have you ever thought about a national prayer walk?" His eyes grew large and incredulous.

"Across the country? Are you nuts? That's crazy!" He flung the words in the air, willing them to take flight, to flee from the inevitable.

"Well, if you do decide to do it, I would go with you," the words escaped from my mouth like some foreign thing feigning a will of its own. I looked behind me to see if someone else had spoken the ill-fated words, but one look at my husband's face assured me that I had been the one who had uttered the unutterable. I had volunteered to accompany him on an epic journey that would require an element of courage and tenacity I had not yet known or been required to know up to this point in my life.

Yes, I had survived my mother's untimely death when I was twelve years old, had worked since I was thirteen, married young, had overcome a complete breakdown in my early thirties, raised five rambunctious kids and homeschooled for fifteen years. Yes, I was a survivor, but this?

A strange smile crept across my husband's face and I could almost see the mental machinery kick into gear. Could we do it?

I remembered our earlier conversations when we had sensed God's leading, but was our decision based on our desires rather than God's? I continued to cry out to God, "Your will not mine be done." But if we were indeed to continue on this journey, I needed God's wisdom to know how I could help Calvin take this step of faith. The stakes were high; the situation seemingly impossible. Should we draw a final line in the sand and go ahead with the reservations or should we postpone the trip and continue to seek out help? Thoughts of disappointing our supporters and failing our Lord assaulted our minds. If we couldn't even overcome this setback in the safety and security of our own home, among those that we loved, how would we ever make it "out there" in the midst of the unknown, among strangers, isolated from the comforts of home?

I pulled the CD, "Comfort for Those Who Are Hurting" from my collection. If anyone was hurting, if anyone needed comforting, it was my husband. Hour after hour the words of the Psalms played over and over as he lay in the twilight, hanging tightly to what remained of his strength. "I am not getting out of this bed until I have a breakthrough"—words so like the blind beggar, calling to Jesus from the side of the road, whose faith brought sight to his blind eyes; echoing the heart cry of the woman with the issue of blood, defying man's and nature's laws to reach out one last time for the One whom she knew could, no *would* be her ever-present help in time of need.

I didn't dare interrupt the eternal battle raging inside that room. Later, drained but filled with a renewed sense of peace, Calvin recounted how God had brought him through to the other side.

As evening waxed into the darkness of night, the words of love and comfort continued to wrap themselves around his heart, bringing healing, whispering words of comfort and love.

When the morning falls on the far-off hill
I will sing to Him, I will praise Him still.
When trials come and my heart is weighed down
With doubt, I will praise Him still.
For the Lord, our God, He is mighty to save me
From the arms of death, from the depths of the grave.
And He gave me life through His perfect will
And by His grace, I will praise His name.

The words crept into Calvin's thirsty soul, pouring healing oil into his parched mind, bringing life to his weak body. The presence of God swept through the room and Calvin barely breathed, for fear God's Spirit would depart.

"Don't leave me, my God, don't pass me by," he whispered into the stillness. Tears of healing relief flowed down his face, washing away the pain and desperation of the past months. Somewhere deep inside, beyond thoughts, beyond even prayer, he knew that he was loved, accepted; equipped to do His Father's will. Whatever that meant, come what may, he would go forth by faith, trusting God to supply whatever he needed to accomplish the task. The journey across our great nation would indeed become a reality.

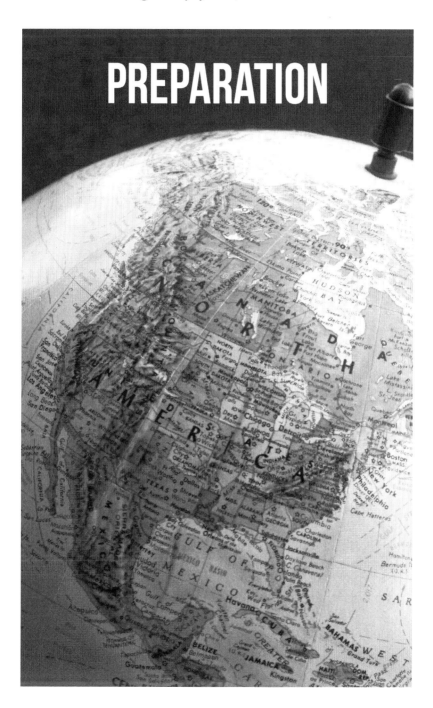

PREPARATION

Counting the Cost
October 2013

Eleven weeks ago we made the decision to embrace the assignment we believe God has given us for the next season of our lives. Walking across the country is not something we decided to do on a whim. Since July 15, when we first discussed the possibility of embarking on this journey, we have sought the counsel of our spiritual leaders and other friends and family whom we trust will speak into our lives in an honest, challenging way.

Are we biting off too much? Can a man of 62 years hold up both spiritually and physically through a grueling six-month intercessory walk of this magnitude? How can we continue to nurture important relationships, maintain our property in Manheim, and continue to meet our financial obligations with both of us on extended leave of absences?

These are just a few of the thoughts and questions that have gone through our minds as we have walked through this initial planning process. Despite our feelings of doubt and inadequacies, God continues to confirm our cross country walk, and many details are falling into place.

By the end of February 2014, two friends, who will be returning from India, have agreed to live in our basement again and will be responsible for the outside upkeep at the house. Their pre-India stay with us went extremely well, and hopefully they anticipate their return to the states with a sense of peace, knowing they have a second home to come back to. Our youngest son will cover home base until they return. Our third daughter has agreed to handle any necessary financial matters and will keep track of our incoming mail. We are still in the process of securing someone to live in the top floor of our home to care for the pets. We have a few options and are trusting God for the perfect "pet lover" to fill this area of need. For those of you who have pets, you know that they are an important part of the family and need love and nurturing while you are away.

On September 22, 2013 we launched our schedule of sharing at interested churches, when we shared our vision and were prayed for at Life Center in Harrisburg. We believe we made some strategic connections at Life Center that God will solidify in the future.

October 6, 2013 we traveled to In the Light Ministries in Philadelphia, where we received some wonderful prophetic ministry, a significant financial donation toward our trip, and most importantly the love and support of the body there. Some of the highlights from what God spoke to us during the service include these promises:

- Connections are already being made for us by the Lord.

- Calvin has a "John the Baptist" anointing upon him for this walk across the nation. As John the Baptist had been called to prepare the way for Jesus, Calvin was going forth to help pave the way for an end times outpouring.

- The Lord will give us strength to finish on time.

- Towns, cities and regions will be touched by the Lord's presence as we go.

- God will give us FAVOR, FINANCES and FAITH.

- We will be carrying the prayers of the people of Philadelphia as well as the heart of the Father to the nation.

Connecting to the Atlantic Ocean
November 2013

We just finished out the month of October and our schedule has been full as we share our vision with different expressions of the Body of Christ. As we visit various churches, we find it interesting to see how each member fulfills its call and mission in releasing the kingdom of God here on Earth. Calvin is completing his last prayer walk of 2013 by walking to the East Coast and finishing at the Atlantic Ocean in Ocean City, New Jersey. It is important to him that we connect the East Coast to the West Coast through prayer and intercession, so we are taking advantage of the seasonal fall weather to put our feet into the chilly waters of the Atlantic. From this point we will carry the prayers and petitions of the believers from the East Coast across the nation to the believers on the West Coast. One body, one church, one Lord—united together in common purpose—to see His kingdom come, His will be done on Earth as it is in Heaven.

We finally made it to the Atlantic Ocean, where Calvin put his feet in the chilly waters. Our vision was to connect the East Coast to the West Coast, both spiritually and physically.

We arrived at the Atlantic Ocean on October 26, 2013. As Calvin was entering the city limits of Ocean City, New Jersey at 1:18 p.m., he was reminded of Psalm 118, verse 8, the middle verse of the Bible, "It is better to put your trust in the Lord than put confidence in man." Upon arriving at the water's edge at 1:36 p.m., the Lord reminded him of Psalm 136. Reading it later that day, he realized with amazement that it was the twenty-sixth day of the month; the chapter had 26 verses, all which end with "His mercy endures forever." Calvin knew he could embrace and carry this truth with him every day of our national prayer walk, from the East to the West.

When we checked into the motel, the man at the front desk "happened" to be reading about the Azusa Street revivals, where a mighty spiritual revival took place in 1906 in a small church on Azusa Street in Los Angeles. This three-year revival went on to spark the modern day Pentecostal Movement. Upon hearing about our upcoming national prayer walk, the motel employee asked Calvin to pray for him!

In February 2014 we will begin our six-month trek across the nation and finish at the Pacific Ocean in Los Angeles, California. We know we will have many more encounters just like the motel incident along the way. Another confirmation God gave us on this walk to the Atlantic, was information on a plaque that I saw along the route. All night Friday night the picture of that plaque stayed with me and on the way home on Saturday, we finally found the bronze plaque standing guard over a small wooded grove. It described the mission of the Methodist Circuit Riders who were so influential in that geographic area in the early 1800's. We knew God wanted us to continue on with their vision, bringing the gospel to that area. We agreed with their prayers that were prayed almost two hundred years ago!

Psalm 107:2-3 says that God has redeemed His people out of the hand of the enemy and gathered them from the east, west, north and south. When we shared at a transformation gathering in Baltimore on October 23, we were given a word that God is sovereignly preparing connections for us across the nation and supernaturally positioning believers for us to meet! Verse 7 reads, "He led them forth by the right way." In many ways we are going "blind" in that we have never traveled many of the roads and highways along our route, so we are trusting God for safe, clear routes for Calvin to walk, and we are looking forward to connecting with God's people along the way!

On October 13, 2013 we shared at a small church in Red Hill, Pennsylvania, where the body is reaching out to their community. The Lord has supernaturally enlarged their thrift store and food pantry ministries and given them favor in the community. Pastor Smith has a dynamic vision for transformation within their area, and he and his congregation are pressing into God for wisdom and breakthrough. What a privilege it is to carry part of their heart's cry with us as we go. Their prayers and support, along with so many others, will help sustain us over the long months of being isolated from the presence of our friends, family and church body.

In many ways we see ourselves as missionaries journeying into the wilderness of our nation's spiritual wasteland, imploring the God of Heaven to pour out His Spirit once more upon our great land. Almost everywhere we share, we receive the same word: that Calvin is like a John the Baptist, going forth to help pave the way for an end times outpouring. Like John, there is a separation and consecration that follows this kind of calling. As his wife, I am still trying to grasp, understand, and embrace all that this calling entails. At home, in the security of our comfortable surroundings, it is easy to disconnect from the realities of that call, but here on the road, I am faced with the depth of what it means to embrace our assignment wholeheartedly.

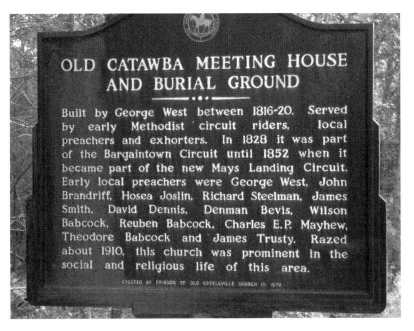

We came upon this plaque on our journey to Ocean City, New Jersey. We joined our prayers with the Circuit Riders' prayers from centuries past.

Sharing the Vision
December 2013

In less than six weeks we will be finalizing last minute details and finishing our packing for our National Cross Walk. Doors continue to open for us to share at various churches. Word of Life in Bensalem, Pennsylvania, is a predominantly Russian church where Calvin preached and we prayed for each person. They prayed that we would be immersed in the spirit of joy and that resources and protection would be granted to us.

On November 17, 2013 Calvin traveled to Emmanuel Church in York, Pennsylvania, where they prayed that he would relate to the humanness of Jesus and that we would have divine connections along our journey. On November 24, 2013 we shared at Cornerstone in Lebanon, Pennsylvania. Through the prayer time, there was an emphasis on sowing into the land, identifying with Johnny Appleseed. They also released the creativity of God over us. November 30 and December 1 found us at our home church, Ephrata Community Church, where we shared our vision, were prayed for, and felt the love and support from our dear friends at our home base. Again, it was proclaimed over us that we would have many connections, specifically with the First Nation's Peoples. December 8 we visited our former church home, Newport DOVE, where we were surrounded by many old friends and family, including my dad, who came to hear Calvin share some of his "Walk Stories."

During the time of preparation, the Lord has been doing some deep inner cleansing in both of us, making these vessels more fit for the Master's use (2 Timothy 2:21). It has not been an easy process as we walk through this time of refining, but we know this is His work, and we just need to yield to the Potter's hand.

Partners in Faith
January 17, 2014

In less than two weeks we will be filling up our bins, packing our suitcases, and bidding a final farewell to our family. After six months of preparation and sharing the vision at churches and through radio and print media, the National Cross Walk vision is becoming a reality. It's time to take all the prayers of faith and gifts of support and begin our journey across this great nation.

A big thank you to everyone who has committed to pray for us during the walk and also to those who have given financially. We have been humbled and encouraged by your support. We believe you will share in the fruits of this walk through your partnership. We welcome you to keep in contact with us over the next six months through the website, email or by phone. Watch for our regular email updates—we know we will have some stories to tell.

"For whoever calls on the name of the Lord shall be saved. How then shall they call on Him in whom they have not believed? And how shall they believe in Him of whom they have not heard? And how shall they hear without a preacher? And how shall they preach unless they are sent?" As it is written in Romans 10:13-15, "How beautiful are the feet of those who preach the gospel of peace, who bring glad tidings of good things!"

Six Days and Counting . . .
January 25, 2014

I just finished reading an update from a dear friend of mine who is grappling with the death of a loved one and who is grieving the loss of her mother's health. Her steadfast faith and trust in our Lord refreshed and inspired me as I have felt overwhelmed with the reality of the journey that lies ahead of us. I realize how totally consuming the doing of life can be; so much so that we lose touch with the deeper meaning that permeates all we do. So here we are hustling and bustling about—preparing for this cross-country prayer walk that we hope impacts the course of our nation's future—yet feeling so shallow, at times disconnected from the source of that impetus. So like the biblical character Martha we are. She had the essence of life in her midst and yet she was so busy doing life, she missed the opportunity to let that life permeate and change her.

In a few short days we will be embarking on a seemingly impossible journey, traversing a country, 3,000 miles wide, that is gasping for life itself, even though the Giver of Life waits patiently to breathe divine life back into it. Like Ezekiel, we look across the valley of dry bones and wonder, how shall these bones live? How will all that the enemy has torn apart and shattered be woven together again? And what is our part to play? To see, to walk, to cry out, to speak for those who have yet to find their voice? What is your part? To see, to cry out, to agree with us for the impossible? Lord help us not to fear, but help us to see that those who are with us are more than those who are with the enemy (2 Kings 6:16).

Our hearts cry out with the words of Mary the mother of Jesus, "For He is mighty who has done great things for me, and holy is His name. And His mercy is on those who fear Him from generation to generation. He has shown strength with His arm; He has scattered the proud in the imagination of their hearts. He has put down the mighty from their thrones and exalted the hungry. He has filled the hungry with good things. . . ." (Luke 1:49-53).

Calvin had these fourteen shepherd's staffs made to present to each state we would have contact with or be passing through on our cross country prayer walk.

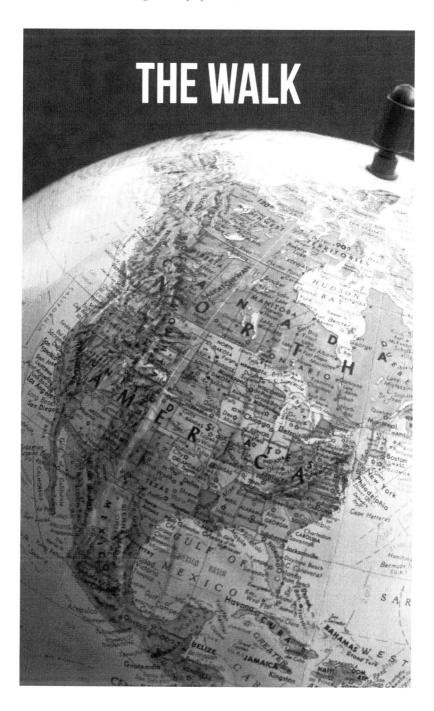

THE WALK

Our Adventure Begins

Our hearts stirred with emotion as we pulled out of our driveway that cold January morning, committing our families, the home we love, and our future into the hands of our loving Heavenly Father. I had over-planned and over-packed (as usual) and we found ourselves emptying containers and leaving various supplies behind at the last minute as we ran out of room in our compact car. Our drive to West Liberty, West Virginia, where Calvin had ended a prayer walk in 2008, was uneventful except for the swirling excitement that permeated our hearts and minds as we began our cross-country adventure.

You'd think we were going cross country or something.

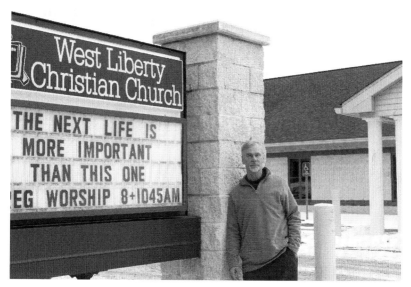

This was the church where Calvin ended his 2008 prayer walk. He had completed walking from the Atlantic Ocean to this location. Now, it was time to continue west.

First stop was West Liberty Christian Church, the tiny community church where Calvin presented a shepherd's staff in 2008. After fellowshipping with two parishioners who were faithfully cleaning the church that day, we phoned the pastor whom Calvin had met six years ago, and he graciously prayed a blessing over us. The day had finally come for us to launch out into the deep and officially begin our national prayer walk the next day.

Saturday dawned bright and seasonably warm for February 1. Early that morning, we discovered a beautiful trail that wound alongside the Ohio River into the city of Wheeling. As Calvin worked his way into the city, I explored the steely city of Wheeling, nicknamed "the Friendly City," which was nestled in the foothills of the Appalachian Mountains. Formally known as a key manufacturing center during the nineteenth century, Wheeling now appeared a shadow of its former glory, with darkened period buildings lining its narrow, worn main street. I was soon captivated by the Wheeling Suspension Bridge, the largest of its kind from 1849-1851. Calvin ended his first day of walking by crossing that majestic bridge into the State of Ohio.

Three nagging questions remained at the end of the day—where would we spend our first Sunday fellowshipping? Who would receive the West Virginia shepherd's staff we had brought along? And how could we give money to the student fellowship of a university, which we had passed while driving the day before?

As Calvin and I relaxed in our hotel room that evening, I flipped on the TV. Immediately, an advertisement for the Wheeling Vineyard Church came on. I knew instantly that was where the Lord wanted us to attend the next morning.

Attending an unfamiliar church in a strange city lends itself to a number of challenges. First, you have to find it—thank God for a GPS. Second, we had no contact person to share our vision with of presenting them with a specially made West Virginia shepherd's staff. And so the two of us, strangers hailing from Pennsylvania, waltzed into the foyer carrying a tall wooden staff and immediately bumped into the pastor himself. After exchanging a few words of greeting, he told us to meet with him between the two morning services. After the first service, we shuffled into his modest office and he signaled for a few of his elders to join us. Huddled together with his wife and small children, we proceeded to share the vision for our cross-country walk and how we believed God led us to that church. As we prayed and released the shepherd's staff to this small faithful church we also released a divine mandate of influence and fruit. Afterwards, the pastor shared with humility on how they had done demographic studies of the entire state and that God had graciously given them strategic insight on how to reach every county in the state with the gospel. We also discovered that the president of the university, where we had felt led to sow financially, actually attended this church. In amazement, we rejoiced together at the mystery of God's ways and His incredible timing. This was just the first of many such God connections that would unfold supernaturally throughout the course of our trip.

Crossing the historic Wheeling Suspension Bridge in Wheeling, West Virginia.

Presenting the West Virginia shepherd's staff at Wheeling Vineyard Church. Chris and Christy Figaretti have a vision to plant a church in every county in West Virginia!

Is Winter Winning?
February 10, 2014

We arrived in Springfield, Ohio this afternoon. I was anticipating another few hours on the phone with technicians trying to figure out why I couldn't send emails from my contact list, when much to my delight the process finally worked. Most of you aren't aware that we have been having major email issues since last week.

It seems like Old Man Winter may have the upper hand right now—roadsides are still snow covered, many sidewalks are still piled high and many of the wonderful Ohio trails are unplowed. We continue to search for walkable streets and roads each day. God led us to some great trails in downtown Columbus, including the Scioto Trail, which runs along the Scioto River and is used by many commuters who walk or bike to work or school in the city each day. Calvin spent part of the day last Friday in Franklin Park walking the park road. It was there that we got an encouraging phone call from a prophetic intercessor from Morning Star Ministries (Rick Joyner's ministry in Charlotte, North Carolina). He shared a dream that involved two eagles; one was almost dead and the other one was taking care of it. The caller said that after praying about the interpretation for some time, the ministry team felt strongly that the dream speaks of the state of our nation, and wanted to pass along the interpretation to us. The caller encouraged us to pray for an anointing for Calvin to speak life into America as we go and to specifically continue in prayer

Franklin Park in Columbus, Ohio. It was five degrees but Calvin was able to walk the snowy roads in this park.

The beautiful United Methodist Church in downtown Columbus.

for our President. On Saturday, Calvin continued to pray along two trails that traversed Columbus.

Yesterday we attended World Harvest Church outside Columbus. There, God supernaturally connected us with several elders and deacons who graciously received the Ohio shepherd's staff and prayed grace and strength for us as we continue our walk.

Today Calvin walked some back roads towards London, Ohio despite the "high" of fifteen degrees. It looks like we have a short reprieve from the winter madness this week since all the storm systems are staying east of us. Unfortunately the many miles of trails that we painstakingly plotted ahead of time are

Calvin was supposed to walk this trail outside London, Ohio, but as you can see, it was still snow-covered, so he walked some back roads into London.

What an awesome time of fellowship we had with the believers at World Harvest Church outside Columbus, Ohio.

Two of the elders at World Harvest Church receiving the Ohio shepherd's staff.

unplowed and too difficult for Calvin to walk. He plans to walk the city of Springfield, Ohio tomorrow and then we will begin our cold southward plod towards Cincinnati.

Last night we met a great college student who was filling in for his brother as a server at a local restaurant. We struck up a conversation with him and discovered he is involved with campus ministry at Ohio State University. We had a wonderful time of sharing our vision with him and encouraging each other in the Lord. We never cease to be amazed at how God orders our steps!

We are in our fourth hotel and have our moving-in-and-out routine down to a science now. We are keeping in contact with our family back home, and are thankful for Skype and our modern day technology that helps us to feel not quite so far away. A little different from our ten months in Africa where it took two weeks for letters to travel back and forth and our only phone contact was from a central line at the city phone company and then, after hours of waiting our turn, we were never guaranteed a connection! My how times have changed for the better!

Keep on Keepin' On
February 18, 2014

Many times in life we get to a point where commitment takes over when novelty abandons us. That is precisely where I find myself this week. The security of home, routine and regular connection with those we love has been stripped away, and with each passing mile the distance widens. And so here is where the commitment, the resounding "yes" to the will of God kicks in. Despite the crappy weather, the lack of accessible trails and roads, the constant uprooting and changes in environment, His constant flow of grace is covering us day by day.

The first two weeks, Calvin struggled with finding his rhythm, and some of the old waves of intimidation and self-doubt threatened at times. Now he is in a flow, praying with more certainty and confidence. I, on the other hand, am wrestling with a curious mixture of isolation, boredom and the need to "nest." Those of you who are women know exactly what I am talking about. Deep within each woman is the desire, and yes even the drive, to make our space personal and inviting. Our homes bear the unique stamp of our soul, expressing our creative energy which draws our family and friends into a safe space. How do I find that place in a myriad of hotels designed for transient passers-by? Hunger for beauty and familiar tokens of the heart flourishes no matter where we find our wandering feet. And so my quest for new-found balance in my ever-changing world continues. I am surrounded by God's expressions of beauty through the majesty of nature and yet my soul cries out for connection and purpose.

As we pass thousands of homes sprinkled throughout this great nation, I constantly wonder—who are all these people? What are their hopes and dreams? How did they come to be in this place? Each property expresses who they are—I see the deep need to have a place to call "home." And yet, this place is not our home, but we keep our eyes on that home that awaits us as children of God! We are but sojourners passing through. May we all hold our connection to this earth with open hands. May He remind us that we are but stewards of all this "stuff" and may our hearts cry with abandon—"Not my will but Yours be done."

This is the beautiful trail that Calvin would have walked all the way into Oregonia, Ohio, but instead he walked Old Clifton Road that day. We had to be ready to change his route at any moment due to weather or road conditions.

While Calvin walked along the beautiful Miami River, I drove to Fort Ancient Indian Mounds. Local Indians created dozens of these mounds over 2,000 years ago—the reason is still unknown. Don't you just love a good mystery?

We had a wonderful time fellowshipping at Eastgate Vineyard Church in Cincinnati with Pastor John Sinclair and his wife, Carol.

What a sight—overlooking the Ohio River on Cliff Road in North Bend, Ohio. This was our last day in Ohio.

Snapshots from the Road
February 24, 2014

I sit here gazing out our hotel window across the sparkling lake where the ducks glide, carefree and unhindered. Our heart cry is to follow our Lord with the same abandon, even as Abraham obeyed when he was called to a place that he would receive as an inheritance, not knowing where he was going (Hebrews 11:8). Such are our feelings as we begin each day—our previous plans and route held before the Lord and many times redirected because of weather, safety and traffic. Every few days we relocate to another "base camp" and formulate the game plan for the next few days. Along the way we learn about the unique history of the area and take a crash course on the lay out of the land, meeting people who are hungry for conversation and who feel real pride in their little corner of the world. As Calvin walks the streets and highways, he senses a special connection to the land and even a sense of ownership. Genesis 13:17 continually rings in our heart. "Arise, walk in the land through its length and its width, for I give it to you."

Following is a snapshot of the last few weeks:

We visited World Harvest Church in Columbus, Ohio, where we presented the Ohio staff to the church. We received a wonderful letter of appreciation this week from Rod Parsley, the apostolic leader there, who blessed our journey and was so appreciative of our gesture of friendship.

February 17, 2014 we visited Eastgate Vineyard Church in Batavia, just east of Cincinnati. We were welcomed by the leadership there and blessed by a wonderful traveling minstrel and preacher who ministered there that morning. We also discovered that Wheeling Vineyard, the church we had visited on February 2, was the church plant that the late Keith Green was targeting to plant right before his untimely death in 1982.

We met a lovely fellow believer at an Olive Garden Restaurant last week. She connected us with her church, Northside Christian Church, New Albany, Indiana. We are looking into the possibility of releasing the Indiana shepherd's staff to their congregation.

Our good friend and fellow intercessor, Perry Gerhart, faithfully blows the shofar by phone and prays over us as we enter each new state.

We have had contact with Morning Star Ministries, located in Charlotte, North Carolina, and Harvest Rock Church in Pasadena, California, where we plan to arrive in July. Many other believers continue to cheer us on and encourage us.

We were refreshed and blessed when we attended Living Waters Church in Shelbyville, Kentucky, where Calvin reconnected with Pastor Stephen Riley, an old friend from Pennsylvania. He and his wife accepted the pastorate there this past summer. My thoughts about Kentucky? Past impressions focused on horses and the underprivileged of the Appalachia area in the eastern part of the state, but we found the believers in this state hungry for the prophetic, hospitable and generous. They are people of prayer who have a heart for their fellow Kentuckians. It's amaz-

View of Little Clifty Falls in Clifty State Park, Madison, Indiana. Calvin spent a whole day walking this beautiful 1,519 acre park.

ing how many preconceived ideas we have of the many cultures that are scattered across our country. These unexpectedly come to the surface as we traverse our diverse nation. No matter how varied the cultures, we find the Body of Christ united and faithfully laboring for the Lord.

Calvin continues to meditate on and proclaim Acts 2 and Joel 2 concerning the salvation of souls, and God's heart to pour out His Spirit and restore all things to Himself. The Lord continues to give Calvin prophetic dreams and insights concerning churches and leaders from the mid-Atlantic region. He stays in close relationship with the apostolic leaders in that area of the country.

Today, as Calvin walked across the bridge from Jeffersonville, Indiana to Louisville, Kentucky, he talked to Perry Gerhart by phone from 11:11 until 11:14 a.m. The scriptures Deuteronomy 11:11-14 came to his heart, specifically verse 12, "A land which the Lord your God cares for: the eyes of the Lord thy God are always upon it, from the beginning of the year even to the end of the year." Perry prayed this scripture over Calvin as he walked today throughout downtown Louisville, the largest city in Kentucky.

The first month of our journey is coming to a close. Would you pray with us that we could speak the Word of God with all boldness (Acts 4:29), and would you stand with us as one heart and one soul (Acts 4:32)? Each new day brings with it challenges and triumphs, loneliness and connection. May the Lord find us content in His will as we continue our journey.

View from our hotel room in Clarksville, Indiana.

The Second Street Bridge that Calvin walked over three times into Louisville, Kentucky. The river is high right now due to the thawing ground and it is covering some walkways and steps into the park.

In the Midst of the Wilderness
February 26, 2014

Today was bitterly cold. We ended up in Harrison-Crawford State Forest and then on to some remote back roads along the Ohio River. We are at the southern-most border of Indiana and can look right over into Kentucky. The land looks so untamed and remote, yet we see houses sprinkled in the midst of this wilderness. I always wonder who would want to live in these places. They must be mountain lovers. I guess I am too urbanized, although I don't see Manheim as being urban. I always feel a little lonely and a bit small when I am in these places. I am not like some people who thrive on being out in the middle of nowhere. There is comfort for me in being in "civilization" where other people hurry about living their busy lives. I wish I could just enter into a place of feeling God in creation, but it's all a little intimidating for me. Now put me by the water, any water, and I feel at home. I have so enjoyed connecting with the great Ohio River these past weeks. The water seems to wash over my soul and sweep through me with a deep sense of peace. I wish we could, like Lewis and Clark, journey on with the river, but tomorrow we start our trek north of the river and into Illinois.

I had no idea when we booked our hotel in Clarksville, Indiana that we would be standing on the very shore where Lewis and Clark met and planned their journey into uncharted western territory. The depth of courage they had and the preparation for such a dangerous feat is so beyond my comprehension. Long before the platting of villages and surveying of roads, this vast virgin

We are always encouraged when we see our nation's symbol of freedom flapping freely in the wind. We walk to see God's people live their lives in allegiance and obedience to the author of freedom!

This is a typical scene that we play out over and over again each time we check into and out of every hotel. Sigh... Thankfully we almost always stay at each hotel between two and five nights.

wilderness was untouched except by the local Native Americans. Here we are today, heading west on paved roads with gas stations and fast food restaurants strategically dotted along our way. All these modern conveniences threaten to sap all the pioneer courage and tenacity out of our souls. I find a deep connection growing within me to the pioneer soul of centuries ago. I pray that we as Christians might plod on with abandon, fearing no earthly threat, but allow our inmost beings to resonate with the land that cries out with groans and labors with birth pangs together until now. "We also groan within ourselves, eagerly waiting for the adoption, the redemption of the body . . . the Spirit helps us in our weakness. For we do not know how to pray as we should, but the Spirit Himself makes intercession for us with groanings which cannot be uttered" (Romans 8:22, 26). May our obedience continue to plow up the fallow ground as we journey on. . . .

The beautiful Sisters of St. Benedict Monastery greeted us in the town of Ferdinand, Indiana. This campus houses one of the largest Benedictine communities of women in the United States. The sisters live the Rule of St. Benedict, a spiritual path of finding God in the circumstances of daily life—something we are all called to, but not always easy to do...

Big With a Capital "B"
March 2, 2014

One thing about undertaking something of this sort is that every day is totally different. It doesn't matter how much we plot and plan, we have no way of predicting what each day will hold. For someone who thrives on structure, this can prove to be quite stressful—unless I keep reminding myself that this is all part of a Big adventure with a capital "B"!

It's funny how most people blossom through routine, from the smallest infant to the seasoned senior living out the golden years. It takes some time to normalize the abnormal and familiarize ourselves with the unfamiliar. Some people pride themselves in living a random life with all its unpredictableness. I'm not sure I'll ever be one of those, but my comfort zone is definitely taking on new dimensions!

Yesterday we visited the Angel Mounds, just southeast of Evansville, Indiana. The State Historic Site is one of several museums and grounds depicting Native American villages. Here, in the 1930s, archeologists explored a 103-acre compound, once filled with a thriving Mississippian culture, and unearthed over 1,500,000 artifacts. The people who lived here a thousand years ago flourished on the land, tilled the soil and lived in harmony with the ebb and flow of seed time and harvest, birth and death. For them, there was no randomness. Life was carefully explained through spiritual connections, rituals, and beliefs.

How far we have strayed from those spiritual roots and how blindly we have stepped with abandon into the mire of humanism and self-absorption. Calvin and I are not living off the land like our Native American forefathers, but living out of a suitcase has its challenges. We thought we'd share with you some of the unique challenges we have faced on the road:

- Some of our roads lead to nowhere or end in gravel with innumerable potholes.
- Hotel toilets threaten to overflow and hallways smell like sewage.
- Refrigerators freeze our food or refrigerators are MIA, causing us to use nature's refrigerator outside our hotel door that in turn tempts the birds or some other incognito little beast to peck or gnaw its way through a Ziploc bag and a plastic container to get to our strawberries.
- Remote controls don't work, lights don't work, bathtubs have no stoppers, inside "heated" pools are ice cold, heaters overheat, water never gets hot, and hotel guests and their dogs holler and howl half the night.

Despite these annoyances, I think of our brethren serving on the field in far-off lands, and I realize how easy our lives really are in comparison. "For our light affliction which is but for a moment, is working for us a far more exceeding and eternal weight of glory, while we do not look at the things which are seen. For the things that are seen are temporary, but the things that are not seen are eternal" (2 Corinthians 4:17-18).

May we all continue to rest our gaze on Him who holds us here and through eternity.

We awoke to a Sunday morning ice storm this morning. It took Calvin twenty minutes and three gallons of hot water to open up our car.

Over 1,000 years ago, the Mississippian people built a protection wall such as this to surround 100 acres of their compound. The outer wall was sixteen-eighteen feet tall and 6,300 feet long and was constructed using a wattle and daub technique.

Praying God's Heart
March 4, 2014

Our world is covered in white again as winter storm Titan swept down across the Ohio Valley this past weekend. Even as the land lay encrusted under a half inch of ice, the world continued to rush by, deadlines and appointments to keep. Calvin and I spent Sunday hunkered down at our hotel, enjoying a day of solitude and reflection. Now that we are evaluating the first leg's half-way mark, how do we calculate and define what the Lord is accomplishing through this walk?

A dear friend from back home wrote, *"We know that God is faithful to move on behalf of our prayers because we are praying His heart. You were sent by God on this mission, so now He will accomplish His desire. Obedience is the key; He does the rest, as we continue to follow His direction."* This speaks directly to how we approach each new day. Where should Calvin walk? How long should he walk? Who are we destined to reach out to each day? Who needs to know God loves them with an everlasting love? We look for opportunities to be His hand extended—to the single mom who works diligently every Sunday cleaning the hotel rooms, while her two little ones are being cared for by her sister at home. We give her a monetary token of our gratefulness since she is making sure our physical needs are met while we live life on the road, and we offer a short time of prayer that she would know and experience the love of her Heavenly Father. We reach out to the passersby on the road, path, at the hotels and in the restaurants—to the drivers who stop and ask Calvin if he needs a ride (I guess it looks peculiar for someone to be walking remote roads in single digit weather in their area). When he declines and shares what he is doing, they are greatly impacted. One fellow-believer even drove back an hour later and gave Calvin a monetary gift towards our walk!

Calvin, while walking between Santa Claus, Indiana and the Lincoln Historic Park, also had a friendly visit from a state policeman. After Calvin showed his identification, the officer thanked him for his service and agreed that our nation definitely needs prayer!

We trust God to lead us in prayer. On February 27, Calvin had a strong impression to pray for President Obama, to bless the day he was born and to release his ongoing destiny and purpose. Later we saw on TV that Obama had opened up about his father, drugs and race in an interview that day. We discovered that President Obama's birthday is August 4, our proposed date to arrive back home.

God continues to speak to Calvin's heart about death and life, and the blessing and cursing that come out of our mouths. He has a new revelation of how important it is to always speak blessing and life in his intercession (Proverbs 18:19, James 3:10-11).

For those of you who would like to follow Calvin's heart, here are a few of the many scriptures God has given him to pray over the last few weeks: John 13:20; Philippians 2:1-12; Acts 4:24-34; Luke 11:1-13; Romans 8:26-28; Matthew 7:7-11; Deuteronomy 11:7-32; 1 John 3:8; Psalm 104; 1 Peter 2:5-9; Hebrews 13:15; Jeremiah 6:16; Revelations 12:10-11.

Let's all lay down our human expectations and receive His with an open heart!

A Trail of Tears
March 11, 2014

Occasionally, on our cross-country walk, we encounter a chapter of our nation's history that is difficult to understand and easy to judge. One of these chapters is the removal of five Native American tribes from their homelands in the southeastern part of our country in the 1830's. Reasons for the forced "relocation" were selfish and yet in the European settlers' minds, justified. They needed the land for growing cotton, a huge money crop that was just coming of age. In their minds, the Native Americans were not a legitimate nation, so the process of freeing millions of acres of rich farmland began without a second thought. Tens of thousands of the Choctaw, Chickasaw, Seminole, Creek, and Cherokee peoples were forced to march in harsh conditions, many times without supplies and food, over 1,200 miles across the Mississippi River to "Indian Territory," now the state of Oklahoma. We happened upon the northern branch of the "Trail of Tears," as the Cherokee referred to it, in southern Illinois. Thousands died along the way, a tragedy we observed first hand when we visited the burial ground at the Campground Cumberland Presbyterian Church outside Anna, Illinois. We traced a three and one-half mile segment of the original path and joined together with other intercessors who had gone before us, identifying with the sins of our forefathers. A great sense of peace came over us as we stood on this hallowed ground. I pictured the heartbroken, weary-to-the-bone travelers as they huddled together against the harsh winter wind. Many died from exposure and starvation during that short time of encampment. What if we had been forced to leave the home that we loved and embark on our journey with few provisions, little food, and no shoes to shield our feet from the frozen ground—knowing that we would never see our homeland again? Our hearts broke for their brokenness and the betrayal that these proud people felt from the European settlers.

Even as I say, "I could never do that to someone," I think of the times when others were hurt at the expense of my ambitions, disappointed at my insensitivities, betrayed by my selfishness. We all have a past blemished with sins of omission and commission.

We know our Lord was walking with these brave sojourners as they marched into their unknown future, just as He is with us as we travel on, often unsure of our way, battered by weather and wind and inconveniences. How thankful we are to know our loved ones wait for us back home and that we will return to a future bright with promise and hope. May we continue to carry in our hearts the knowledge that many around us do not have the same assurance as we—an eternity with a loving Heavenly Father. Let's all look for opportunities to be a light and salt in a dark and tasteless world.

We enjoyed our Sunday morning of fellowship at Heartland Christian Center in Carbondale, Illinois. Calvin presented Craig and Gina Hostetler and the congregation with the Illinois shepherd's staff. They are just starting their outreach to the homeless in the area.

It took some searching but we finally located the Trail of Tears route. What a tragic chapter of our nation's history.

We spent some time remembering, praying and grieving over the senseless deaths of these innocent victims that were abruptly forced from their homes. They are not forgotten even though they lie in unmarked graves.

In this church cemetery lie many victims of the forced relocation of 1,500 Cherokee Indians from their homeland in the Carolinas in 1836. Trail of Tears was the name given to the route they traveled passing through Southern Illinois en route to Oklahoma.

This was the breath-taking view from the top of Bald Knob Pass looking out over the Mississippi Valley.

We took a ¾ mile hike down to see the Little Grand Canyon in Shawnee National Forest. We were a bit disappointed when we got to the end of the first trail- we couldn't find any rock formations. The mountain ridges were beautiful, but how much more stunning they would be when painted with a palette of autumn leaves? Tomorrow we leave the forest behind and head north and west toward St. Louis.

A Catalyst for Change
March 16, 2014

Thursday we arrived in St. Louis, Missouri known as the Gateway to the West. It was here that the Lewis and Clark Expedition made its final preparations for the treacherous journey across the western wilderness. Their discoveries made it possible for commerce to continue on to the West Coast and it sparked opportunities for pioneers who dreamed of prosperity and freedom.

St. Louis is also the home of the tragic Dred Scot Decision, where the United States Supreme Court handed down its infamous 1857 decision, stating that African Americans, whether slave or free, could not become citizens of the United States. Rather than deciding the fate of slavery "once and for all," this historic decision fueled the fire for abolitionists in the North and strengthened their call for freedom and justice for all. It quickly became a catalyst for the Civil War.

As we continue our own journey across this great land, we pray that our obedience and continued intercession will also ignite a fire—but this one of the Refiner's fire. We cry out with fellow believers we meet—let us be a catalyst for repentance and revival—not of division and destruction. 150 years ago, the enemy chose Missouri as an example of prejudice and defeat. Today, we pray that it will shine as a beacon of unity, hope and freedom.

Friday, Calvin walked with a friend in East St. Louis, a city known for violence, drugs, and gangs. We know there are giants in the land (Numbers 13:22-33; 14:24), but as God's children, we are to believe a good report (Isaiah 53:1; Romans 10:16; Hebrews 11:2).

Each day we are reminded in Acts 9:31 to have peace, be edified, and walk in the fear of the Lord and in the comfort of the Holy Spirit. Then we will see the Kingdom of God grow and flourish! We carry Psalm 126 in our hearts—"When the Lord brought back the captivity of Zion; we were like those who DREAM. Then our mouth was filled with laughter, and our tongue with singing, then they said among the nations, 'the Lord has done great things for them.' The Lord has done great things for us, and we are glad." Acts 2:16-18 says, "Young men shall see visions and old men shall dream dreams." We pray God would give us His dreams each day!

Calvin continued to sow seeds in the Spirit as he walked throughout the city of Carbondale, Illinois three days this past week, where 20,000 students attend the Southern Illinois University. Most of the students were gone on spring break so he traversed the huge, quiet campus and prayed for the light of the gospel to shine bright in the midst of these young people who are seeking knowledge and direction in life. In Murphysboro he met a man who had lost his wife and daughter, but is serving God in the midst of his loneliness and grief. As they prayed together and embraced as brothers, Calvin knew he would see his new friend in heaven one day.

Each day, no matter where we are, we look for ways to be a blessing to our fellow sojourners. We realize we will never see these people again, so we try to brighten their day and let them know they have purpose and destiny. We are trusting God to open doors for us that no man can shut and to keep closed those doors that are not for us to walk through. John 10:3-4 says we know His voice, we hear His voice, and we follow Him and His voice. May your ears be open to hear Him speaking and may doors of blessing and abundance be yours as you continue to partner with us. . . .

This amazing Arch can be seen for miles as you get closer to St. Louis.

2014 is the 250th birthday of St. Louis. These" birthday cakes" could be found scattered around the city.

The staff at the Jackie Joyner-Kersee Center who faithfully serve the disadvantaged youth of East St. Louis.

We couldn't leave this grand old city before we explored the Old Courthouse, site of the infamous Dred Scott case that shockingly set the course for the Civil War.

Come let us Worship and Bow Down
Psalm 95:6

The day was proving to be a teaser of the long-awaited spring season, winter having dug its claws deeply into the core of the Midwest. "The harshest winter in 25 years" was echoed at dining room tables, in news rooms and inside frozen cars as locals navigated through the rem-

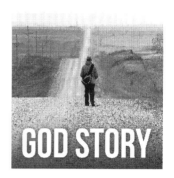

nants of snow and ice left mockingly behind as Old Man Winter reluctantly disappeared. Calvin had been walking the Katy Trail for four days now, weaving his way through the state of Missouri. The 240-mile recreational trail, once the route for the Missouri-Kansas-Texas Railroad, wound its way along the northern bank of the Missouri River.

After weeks of trudging along frigid streets and sidewalks piled high with snow, the "Katy," with her limestone pug cloak, was a joy and delight to Calvin who was hungry for signs that nature would once again awaken from her frozen slumber. Buds were just beginning to show their rounded heads on some of the tree branches and the first courageous spring wildflowers were reaching up towards the March sun. It was March 17, and we found our way to Weldon Springs Trail Head, where he started his day's walk on the flat, dark trail, bordered by rich Missouri farmland sporting short, green winter wheat. His days were filled with sweet fellowship with the Lord and as of yet had not been interrupted by the hikers and bikers that would soon fill this first of its kind Rails-to-Trails recreational trail. Prayers of praise and petition for the local area rose in cadence to the crunching sound of his feet as he strode briskly on. Birds frisked overhead, dancing between the clouds, and joined his song of praise as they chirped skyward, praising their Creator with abandon. Overwhelmed with God's presence, Calvin fell to his knees in worship, lifting his hands, as he was overcome by the goodness and majesty of His God. Calvin's praises echoed through the valley to the God who was worthy of all glory and honor. What a privilege to come willingly, without timidity to the throne of grace. What an honor to freely worship the One who had painted this masterpiece of creation before Calvin's eyes. As he often does when he has a significant spiritual experience, Calvin checked his watch to note the time as he stood to his feet. To his amazement, it was exactly 3:17 p.m.—matching exactly the date on the calendar. God was once again confirming Calvin's call and was receiving the child-like worship of one of His sons. With a renewed sense of purpose, Calvin set his face like flint and marched on towards the western horizon.

Spring Has Finally Sprung!
April 1, 2014

We are beginning to see telltale signs of spring in Missouri—bees are buzzing, bluebirds are busy building nests, caterpillars are on the move, minnows are swimming with renewed energy, butterflies are taking wing, and Calvin joyously spotted his first two turtles sunning themselves beside a bridge. These days of warm spring breezes are a welcome relief from the biting winter cold that we have encountered during most of our trip so far (Psalm 8; 19:1; 104). While enjoying all these hints of spring, on March 20, Calvin asked the Lord to show him just one bird's nest. Later that day, while walking under a bridge, Calvin looked up and stumbled back in astonishment. There were hundreds of swallow's nests, side by side, one on top of the other! The scripture Ephesians 3:20 jumped into his heart. "Now unto Him that is able to do exceedingly, abundantly, above all that we ask or think, according to the power that worketh in us."

Last weekend was full of fellowship with a dear friend, Vanessa, who has recently relocated back to St. Louis and works in an underprivileged school, where she ministers the love of God to fifth graders hungry for love and affirmation. For dinner we connected with another friend, Sheri McCumber from Lebanon, who was visiting a friend in the area. Sunday we fellowshipped at North Church in Florissant, Missouri, where the believers are reaching out to their neighborhood which is fraught with economic and demographic challenges. The Lord put the Mayor of St. Louis on Calvin's heart and he spent a lot of time praying for him while in the area. We entrusted the Missouri shepherd's staff to Pastor Maxedon, the pastor of North Church, and the other elders. We are praying that God would open a door of opportunity for the staff to one day be presented by the area believers and business men and women to the mayor in this strategic city.

What a joy it is for Calvin to continue to walk the Katy Trail this week. This time brought a much-needed break from the vigilance and noise that comes with walking along well-traveled byways and back roads. As always, we met some interesting people, and shared our vision to prayer walk across the country. One family, the Blakes, who were biking the Katy Trail during spring break, helped us with a lost Beagle puppy that we had found on the trail. This adorable nine-month old Beagle followed this family for miles until they contacted police for assistance. If the dog wasn't claimed within 24 hours, the Blake family planned to adopt the spunky little fellow.

We also met a wonderful Christian family, the Pinneys, who were enjoying the warm spring day. We prayed and encouraged each other to continue on in the faith. They are fans of the International House of Prayer in Kansas City where we will be spending a day in April.

At our hotel in Columbia, Missouri, we met several believers who were in the area to attend the State High School Basketball Play-offs in the city. The Christian Brothers' College High School won the Class 5 State Championship, and Calvin had an opportunity to congratulate the head coach who gave God all the glory for their victory. While walking the streets of Columbia, Calvin met two women who were praying outside an abortion-providing clinic. On one of the busiest streets in the city, Calvin joined them in praying for abortion to end in our nation. These experiences constantly remind us that we are investing in people, and that we live by faith and not by sight (2 Corinthians 4:16-18; 5:7). We continue to sow seeds into many people day by day and we are expecting eternal fruit.

As Calvin walks and prays he realizes that it is the enemy's plan to seek whom he may devour (1 Peter 5:8), but Jesus came to seek and save those who are lost (Luke 19:10). He also understands the grace of God on a deeper level, which is the power and ability of Jesus to do God's will (1 Corinthians 15:10; Ephesians 2:8).

We spent our day off on March 15 with our good friend Vanessa Fisher, who served as a fifth grade teacher at a local school. It was great to be with a friendly, familiar face.

It was a joy to spend time praying with our friends in St. Louis. Calvin loved being surrounded by these four lovely women.

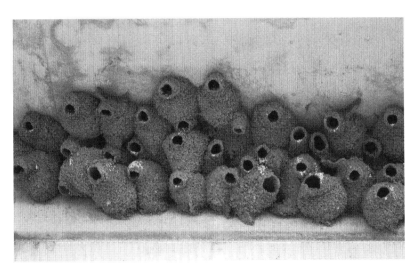

When Calvin asked God to see one bird nest, this is what God surprised him with. God gives above and beyond what we can ask or think!

What a wonderful break it was for Calvin to be able to walk the Katy Trail through the first half of Missouri. I could drop him off and pick him up at the trail heads each day which made my job easier.

Sights like this greeted Calvin each day as he walked "The Katy" through the rural areas of Missouri.

The Katy Trail runs the width of the state of Missouri, starting in St. Charles and ending in New Franklin, Missouri. Calvin was able to walk one hundred miles of this famous trail.

We met the Pinney's at the Rocheport Trail Head on the Katy Trail. I noticed Mr. Pinney's shirt with a scripture on it and we bonded immediately. They have been to International House of Prayer in Kansas City where we will spend a day in April. They also talked about different parts of the city of Columbia that need prayer. They are agreeing with us for revival in this area!

Sowing Seeds of Love and Hope
April 10, 2014

With some hesitancy I began the second leg of our National Cross Walk. Knowing what lies ahead brings both comfort and apprehension. Our brief ten-day "touchdown" back home rekindled familiar sights, sounds and the warmth of family hugs and companionship—just enough to wet the drought of my lonely soul. Once again, a time of release and surrender is at hand, knowing those we hold closest are miles away yet living always in our hearts. Ahead are seven more weeks of new "homes," traversing unfamiliar land and befriending strangers who soon become new friends—another season for opening our hearts to new paths, knowing our Lord has gone before us.

Our call to sow seeds of love and hope continually rings in our hearts. How many times have we been given the analogy of Johnny Appleseed? Romantic legend paints the image of him randomly spreading seeds wherever he traveled. In reality, he was a trained nurseryman who planted nurseries rather than orchards. These nurseries were nurtured, had fences built around them, and were left in the care of skilled gardeners.

Our prayer is that the seeds that we sow would not be haphazardly thrown to the wind but strategically sown, and that God would raise up faithful sons and daughters to water and nurture the seeds until their appointed time of fruition.

John Chapman (the real-life Johnny Appleseed) was also a passionate missionary who converted many Native Americans to the faith. He was loved and respected wherever he went. During this second leg, we desire to be faithful representatives of a good and holy God and not grow weary in well-doing.

During our first break at home, the Lord impressed on Calvin's heart the following hymn that so eloquently shares our heart cry:

"Sowing in the morning, sowing seeds of kindness, sowing in the noontide and the dewy eve; Waiting for the harvest, and the time of reaping, we shall come rejoicing bringing in the sheaves.

CHORUS: Bringing in the sheaves, bringing in the sheaves, we shall come rejoicing, bringing in the sheaves.

Sowing in the sunshine, sowing in the shadows, fearing neither clouds nor winter's chilling breeze;

By and by the harvest, and the labor ended, we shall come rejoicing, bringing in the sheaves.

Going forth with weeping, sowing for the Master, Tho' the loss sustain'd our spirit often grieves;

When the weeping's over, He will bid us welcome, we shall come rejoicing, bringing in the sheaves."

Today we spent the day worshipping and soaking in God's presence at the Kansas City International House of Prayer. We felt our hearts renewed for the task ahead and were encouraged by the university students who are sending out twelve teams this spring to major universities and cities around the nation. Along with us, the students' prayers are for revival amongst this generation. Tomorrow, Calvin will begin his walk through Kansas in the city of Olathe. We will be following the Santa Fe Trail, and working our way towards New Mexico. We say with the Psalmist, "Show me your ways, O Lord; Teach me your paths. Lead me in Your truth and teach me, for You are the God of my salvation" (Psalm 25:4-5). May you find joy as you sow love in your little corner of the world!

We spent our first day of the second leg at the Kansas City International House of Prayer. We spend six hours basking in the presence of God during their 24/7 worship service. It had been over ten years since we visited IHOP- it was good to be back.

Count Zinzendorf, founder of The Moravian Church, started a hundred yearlong prayer meeting. Many missionaries were sent out of this early movement. Leviticus 6:13 commanded the Israelites to keep the fire on the altar burning. The International House of Prayer has adopted this mandate. This spring their university is sending out twelve teams to evangelize a number of major universities and cities around the nation.

Potholes!
April 17, 2014

Our first week back on the road has definitely been filled with some "potholes"—we discovered we had left two strategic map books at home; we experienced severe storms that brought snow and temperatures in the twenties; I slipped in the shower, and although I ended up outside the shower on the tile floor, I had no significant bruising; I came down with some kind of flu and was laid up for three days; an important part of our septic system back home needed repair. So much for an easy start to our second leg! We are constantly reminded that we can do nothing without God's strength and grace —"For our light affliction, which is but for a moment, is working for us a far more exceeding and eternal weight of glory, while we do not look at things which are seen, but at the things which are not seen. For the things which are seen are temporary, but the things which are not seen are eternal" (2 Corinthians 4:17-18).

On a positive note, God redeemed our negligence in leaving our maps behind. He led us to an AAA office where we learned of a sixty-mile trail not far from our proposed route. Aptly named The Flint Hills Nature Trail, this rugged trail is the seventh longest in the nation and lies on an old railroad bed. The trail is scattered with flint stone, a hard sedimentary rock that was used for millennia to make tools. (Isaiah 50 tells us that Jesus set his face like flint when faced with the agonies of the cross). Calvin is enjoying being on a trail again where he is free to focus on prayer and worship and is not distracted by road traffic.

We will be in Kansas until May 11, so we will spend more time in this state than any other. History tells us how Kansas was the traditional gateway to the "wild, wild west" and so has a rich history of ruffians and trouble makers. As in many other mid-western states, the history of Indian resettlement and confiscation of their native land paints broad strokes of injustice across the canvas of Kansas history. Since we will be spending so much time in this state, we thought you might enjoy some little known Kansas trivia:

- A grain elevator in Hutchinson is a half mile long and holds 46 million bushels in its thousand bins.

- Dodge City is the windiest city in the United States.

- At one time it was against the law to serve ice cream on cherry pie in Kansas.

- Smith County is the geographical center of the 48 contiguous states.

- A monument to the first Christian martyr on United States Territory stands along Highway 56 near Lyons. Father Juan de Padilla came to the region with the explorer Coronado in 1541.

- The Hugoton Gas Field is the largest natural gas field in the U.S.

- There are more than 528 caves in Kansas.

- The Geodetic center of North America is about forty miles south of Lebanon at Meade's Ranch. It is in the beginning point of reference for land surveying North America. When a surveyor checks a property line, he or she is checking the position of property in relation to Meade's Ranch in northwest Kansas.

As always, your love and support mean so much as there are times when we feel isolated and alone while on the road. We love hearing from you and hope our regular updates help you feel as if you are here with us.

Calvin discovered the rugged, isolated Flint Hills Nature Trail that runs sixty miles from Osawatomie to Herington, Kansas.

Yesterday he walked eighteen miles on The Flint Hills Nature Trail, passing through several towns and did not see one soul. While some people would be uncomfortable with this degree of solitude (yours truly included), it is the perfect "space" for Calvin to stay focused in prayer and worship.

These stones are scattered all across the trail. Here is an example of their unique colors and diverse qualities.

Although the scenery in Kansas is nothing to write home about (mostly grasses, shrubs and scruffy growth) you can always count on a good colorful sunset to lift your spirits.

The Winds Blow
April 21, 2014

Kansas is known for its changeable and sometimes volatile weather and is a "Tornado Alley" state. According to AccuWeather officials, the tornado season has been quieter than normal to date this year, for which we are very thankful. The winds continually whip into Kansas due to the Rocky Mountains being relatively close by. On many days, Calvin has walked into 20 to 40 mile per hour winds. We are experiencing a drought in central Kansas with only 1.85 inches having fallen on this dry and thirsty land since January 1. One farming couple Calvin met last week asked him to please pray for rain for this area. We are trusting God for at least three inches—without the severe weather that often accompanies heavy rain here. Yes, we knew we were in Kansas when we started to see "Tornado Shelters" for sale alongside the road!

After almost a week of me being down with the flu, we are launching into this new week with a renewed appreciation for health and strength that we need every day in order to fulfill this vision. A special thank you to all of you who prayed for me last week. Having to see a strange health care provider and recuperate far from the familiar sights, sounds and comforts of home is a challenge. As best as he could, Calvin carried on with his walking across many miles of gravel and dirt roads throughout our heartland.

Yesterday we celebrated Easter in Hesston, Kansas at Kingdom Life Ministries, pastored by Scott Miller. We were blessed by the ministry of Sergio and Kathleen Scataglini, a precious couple from Louisiana, who were special speakers for the weekend. We really connected with the believers and felt the Kansas shepherd's staff should be given to this church. The presentation confirmed their mandate from the Lord to continue to expand their vision statewide. Since the church is connected to the Hopewell Network, Pastor Miller and his wife have connections with many ministers from our local area. We fellowshipped and enjoyed lunch together and talked into the afternoon about vision for this vast prairie state.

Calvin continues to receive daily assignments from the Lord and meets and shares our vision with the locals as we plod along. A prophetic word given to him by a precious brother in 2009 continues to ring in Calvin's heart day after day as he prays, and he wanted to share it with all of you:

> *"Another year has now come and passed,*
> *you sowed things that surely will last.*
>
> *You've gone where I've sent you many a time,*
> *sometimes easy and at times a difficult climb.*
>
> *Many footsteps taken to further My plan,*
> *My kingdom expanded by an obedient man.*
>
> *Where are we going this year, My son?*
> *Are you still willing to see battles won?*
>
> *Are you still looking for my kingdom to grow?*
> *Are you still willing to go wherever I go?*
>
> *Is your life still Mine to use as I will?*
> *Is your sword still Mine for a strategic kill?*

Is your heart still crying for Me to appear?
Is your life still Mine for yet another year?

Answer Me slowly, think on what you say,
the cost continues to be all you can pay.

The choice is still yours to stay or to yield;
count the true cost of laboring in My field.

If you can give Me your all, I'll give you Mine too;
I'll continue to sow in you things that are true.

I'll increase your anointing and strengthen your arm,
I'll protect you and yours from the enemy's harm.

Don't look to how I've used you before;
I'll now take you through a different door.

Your feet will still take you to places for me;
Your anointing will still cause the enemy to flee.

Your heart is still the messenger of My love;
My spirit will still give you strength from above.

But listen closely to what I'll now say to you,
a Commander's voice yet still gentle and true.

The battle is increasing but so is My grace;
hold to my Word and look into my face.

I will increase in you a listening heart;
a home for My truth that I will impart.

So another year begins, My warrior son;
Let's run to the battle until it is won.

Take my hand and together we'll fight;
until the darkness is turned into light.

Until the captives have all been set free;
until every heart belongs to Me."

We know many of you continue to pray for us and hold us up to our Heavenly Father. Know that your prayers are felt and appreciated. We pray that your load will be easy today and your burden light and that you'll stay true to the high calling on each one of your lives. May the winds of His Spirit envelope you and may grace fall like rain in your life today!

On Easter morning we had the privilege of presenting the Kansas shepherd's staff to Pastor Scott Miller (on right) at Kingdom Life Ministries in Hesston, Kansas. We were touched by the ministry of Sergio Scataglini from Louisiana that morning.

Easter sunrise—He is risen indeed!

Lessons From the Past
April 28, 2014

Today is cloudy and cooler, which is a welcome relief after several days in the eighties and nineties here on the Central Plains. Severe storms continue to spring up all around us, but we have skirted them so far. Conversation about the weather constantly surrounds us, since every year hundreds of people are killed by deadly twisters that pop up quickly across the area. This year not one person has been killed by severe storms. Each day we commit the weather and our safety to the Lord, since Calvin has nowhere to take cover while walking the remote, flat gravel/dirt roads.

Saturday was our "field trip" day as we visited the local zoo, the Santa Fe Trail Interpretive Center and Fort Larned, an outpost on the remote Santa Fe Trail in the 1800's, from which military men escorted commercial travelers across sometimes hostile Native American territory. We also stopped at Pawnee Rock, which looms fifty feet above the prairie and served as the halfway point along the 800 mile long Santa Fe Trail. We came away with a greater understanding and respect for those courageous pioneers who left everything they knew and loved to begin a new life in this untamed, harsh wilderness. Because few trees can be found across the central plains, many pioneers lived in sod homes, built with the dust of the prairie. They began their new lives with the few belongings they were able to bring along with them from the East. Surviving violent storms, brush fires and hostile Native Americans, the pioneers went on to build our mid-west into the thriving agricultural and oil-producing region it is today.

While walking west of town on Saturday, Calvin met some fellow believers from Faith Community Church, a charismatic church in Great Bend. Sunday morning we enjoyed a wonderful time of fellowship with them in their morning service. Everywhere we go we find faithful followers of Jesus who are praying for our nation's restoration and are making a real impact in their communities. We finished off our day by visiting the Cheyenne Bottoms, one of the world's most important wetlands. Here, more than sixty-thousand acres of wetlands host millions of migrating birds each year. We passed through the small town of Claflin, where Main Street boasts renovated storefront facades to resemble Claflin in the 1890's. By mid-afternoon the hazy horizon was awash with the prairie dust being kicked up by the fifty miles per hour winds.

Today Calvin begins another week of prayer walking filled with petitions for both our nation as well as the local areas we are passing through. Tomorrow we head down to Dodge City, once called "the Wickedest Little City in America." We will continue our trek southwest towards the Panhandle of Oklahoma, where we will arrive May 12. God continues to show Himself faithful on our behalf as we approach the halfway point in our walk this week.

The following scriptures have been important to Calvin over the last weeks and months and he meditates on and declares them as he walks: Luke 11:1-13; 1 Thessalonians 5:17; Romans 8:26-28; Ephesians 6:18; 1 Corinthians 14: 2,4,14-15; Jude 20.

This is what Calvin looks at each morning as he sets off on his daily walk here in Kansas. The road seems to stretch forever out in front of him. As you can imagine, he sees very few cars and those he does see are mostly pick-ups; farmers traveling along their vast fields. He finds it much easier to concentrate and stay in the spirit of prayer on these long, lonely days.

We see windmills like this dotting the barren fields which will soon be alive with thousands of acres of hearty wheat. Scenes like this remind us of home in Lancaster County...

Thousands of head of cattle graze across the miles of pasture here in central Kansas. There are several famous cattle trails nearby where for years, herds of cattle were driven out across the wind-swept prairie. When Calvin walks by, they all scurry to see him close up. I guess it adds some excitement to their otherwise boring existence. One rancher told Calvin there had been "some trouble up north" referring to some unwelcome cattle rustling that had recently taken place. Calvin assured him he's anything but a cattle rustler!

Working oil wells are a familiar sight all across the prairie. Crude oil is a very important commodity in this part of the country. Calvin can often smell the crude as he walks along the back roads.

Throughout the town of Great Bend, you can find these beautiful murals painted on the sides of buildings that tell about the unique history and culture here in the mid-west.

Sights like this remind us that spring is really here to stay.

This natural stone outcropping might not look like much to Easterners, but to the pioneer on the open plains, this landmark, which could be seen for miles, signaled that they were half way to their destination in Santa Fe.

I was looking forward to seeing the Santa Fe Trail Center in Larned, Kansas for weeks. They had an extensive collection of artifacts from the 1800's and gave us a clear picture of what the travelers on the Santa Fe Trail experienced.

Due to the lack of trees on the plains, those who settled in Kansas often lived in sod homes which were cheap and quick to build. These pioneers were often plagued by rodents, leaking roofs and constant, unrelenting dirt.

Soldiers and visitors to Fort Larned left their indelible mark by carving their names into the sandstone used to build the fort. The oldest known dated "signature" was carved by R.R. Hein in May 1877. The fort was built in 1859.

We had a wonderful time of fellowship with Pastor Sandy and Joe Kennedy from Faith Community Church in Great Bend.

A graceful Blue Heron, airborne over the vast Cheyenne Bottoms Marsh just north east of Great Bend.

In the Midst of the Storm

The cold and snow of winter had reluctantly moved on and the incessant westerly winds were more than happy to take their place. Legend has it that some early settlers, who had forsaken the comforts and familiarity of life in the East, were driven mad by the relentless howling

of the Kansas winds. Each evening we listened carefully to the local forecasts, praying the winds would be less of a factor for the next day's walk.

We awoke early, Calvin weary from the previous day's walk. His legs were stiff and uncooperative from bracing himself against the constant winds that buffeted him without mercy. Our hearts sank as the alert flashed across the TV screen—wind advisory, fifty mile per hour winds expected. We double checked our route for the day and decided he would walk a main highway down to the famous Pawnee Rock, the half-way mark for pioneers traveling west on the Santa Fe Trail from Missouri. Standing guard over the open prairie, where millions of buffalo once roamed, the edifice was an important lookout for Native Americans through the centuries.

I dropped him off at his starting point, five miles from our hotel, with the plan to pick him up six hours later at our set meeting point. Unknowingly I had dropped him at the wrong road; an oversight that more than likely saved his life later that day. That afternoon I would hear how God had brought him safely through the midst of the storm.

The winds crept up stealthily that morning, growing gradually into an unruly force, defying man and beast. As it whipped into intermittent frenzies, Calvin was forced to shield his face from the onslaught. He knew if he continued on his current westerly course he would be facing the full force of the storm. He conceded defeat and decided to veer north and head back towards town. In the distance the sky turned fuzzy and his visibility quickly diminished. Should he turn back; make a run for it? He pulled his camera from his sling. If he was going to get caught in this thing, he might as well document it.

Dust storms are common in this part of the country. From the devastating Dust Bowl in the 1930's to the present day dust storms, locals are familiar with the unyielding waves of homeless earth that dance through the sky with little warning or remorse. At its height, the dust storm resembled a dense fog but painted the air a sickly green, coating cars and buildings with a grimy cloak. Kansas was in the midst of a five-year drought, and conditions were perfect for a debilitating dust storm.

The clouds of dirt came in waves with brief spurts of relief, giving him just enough time to get his bearings. There were no vehicles on the road save a few courageous truckers who refused to relent to the foul weather. And then in the distance Calvin saw it—the granddaddy of the dust waves bearing down upon him. He slowed to a crawl, ducked his head and began snapping pictures as the airy arms of debris wrapped themselves around him. He felt all there was in the world was the screeching of the wind and the endless dust. He stood glued to the spot, waiting for his escape. Eventually the air cleared enough for him to spot a narrow trail that headed in the direction of the hotel, where safety and clean air waited.

What a relief to arrive back at the hotel in one piece. He was covered in dark brown soot, the left side of his face appeared as if someone had camouflaged him for nighttime espionage. News came that the main highway, where he had planned to walk, had been completely shut down. There had been several car accidents and one tragic fatality. How could I have even gotten to him in the midst of that storm had he been on the right road? Miraculously, God was turning even our mistakes around for good. Even the destructive winds of the parched plains couldn't blow us off the course that God had for our journey.

While walking toward Pawnee Rock, Calvin got caught in this dust storm.

If he was going to get caught in a dust storm, Calvin thought he would at least document it.

This is what Calvin looked like after several hours of walking in the intense wind and getting caught in a dust storm.

My God Shall Supply

Our home base for the week was the quaint Kansas town of Hesston. It is a lazy prairie hamlet whose premiere resident is a small Christian college that is spread over half the town. Even though there are roads every mile, running predictably towards the western horizon, most ran  due west and we were on a south-westerly trajectory. It was our sixth day in the area, so Calvin was venturing further and further from our hotel, off into the wide expanse of the prairie, working his way towards Hutchinson, the nearest mid-size city.

Today, sixteen miles of Road G was to be his companion. The course sienna gravel road is cornered by dull prairie fields. Since arriving in Kansas, our visual stimulation had been sorely lacking the past few weeks. Calvin found that the vast mid-west cloud formations fascinated and intrigued him throughout his long hours of trudging ever onward towards the southwest border of the state. The theater in which they danced yawned large and endless, much like the ceilings of the planetariums where spectators gape in amazement at the boundless borders of the universe. Calvin reached for his trusty compact camera that documented his walk each day. Many pictures told his personal story of struggles, victories and times of revelation and fellowship with the Lord. Due to its heavy use during the past month, the camera had chewed up quite a few batteries. As Calvin pushed the "ON" button, nothing

. . . not a sound. Being too far from the hotel, with no store in sight for at least twenty miles, he resigned himself to the fact that today's events would be undocumented; today his brain would have to be the instrument that captured the memories of the day.

His prayers were flowing now and he was enjoying another day of praying for the region, trusting that God would hear and answer his petitions. He glanced to the left, and there by the side of the road was a bright purple piece of plastic. The bright color caught his eye and he walked closer to investigate. He was used to finding objects of every imaginable shape, size, and condition on his prayer walks—Bibles, toys, clothing, tools—you name it, he had found it. Bending down he noticed three worn batteries sticking out of the broken plastic. No . . . could it be? They were the exact size that he needed for his camera. The chances of the batteries still in working condition were slim, but why not, he'd give it a try. He cleaned off the batteries the best he could, and opening the camera, he slipped the batteries in place.

Why should he be surprised that they worked, hadn't he experienced this kind of supernatural provision many times? Years ago, during one local prayer walk, Calvin had expressed to the Lord how hungry he was for an apple. Immediately he looked to his left and spotted a ripe apple gleaming at the side of the road. Coincidence, happenstance? Calvin knew that God had heard his prayer and given him the desire of his heart. Many times our financial needs had been met just at the right time—not usually early, but God was never late.

The camera buzzed to life and Calvin laughed at the sheer absurdity of the whole thing. In all his thirty years of prayer walking, he had never seen old batteries alongside the road. Of all the roads he had decided to walk that morning, it had to be Road G, although he could have chosen dozens of others instead. He was on the right road, looking at the right spot along the roadside, at exactly the right time. "Therefore do not be like them. For your Father knows the things you need of before you ask" (Matthew 6:8). God was indeed going before us, guiding our way, and lavishing His provision on us, before we even knew what we needed.

After Calvin's camera batteries inconveniently died, he spotted this discarded toy alongside the road. Miraculously, the batteries were the exact size he needed and they worked!

Halfway
May 3, 2014

The cold and snow of the first leg of our journey has given way to heat, wind and dust. It looks like we will be experiencing record high temperatures over the next five days. The air is hot and dry, and up until yesterday we were fighting twenty-five to fifty mile per hour winds. You may ask why I talk about the weather so much. In the normal course of our lives we could skirt around the foul weather and commiserate from either our workplace or from the comfort of our climate-controlled home. Calvin doesn't have that luxury as he interacts with the forces of nature in a very intimate way each day. Deciding what to wear, what time of the day to walk in order to bypass bad weather and shoring himself up against the elements day in and day out is his daily reality. I have been blessed to be back at the hotels much more during this leg, but I often take him to his starting point in the morning and pick him up at the end of his day. The countless dirt roads he walks are filled with unforeseen adventures. He came upon a bull snake sleeping at the side of the road one day this week, which alarmingly resembles a western rattlesnake. A friendly dog, Stan, followed Calvin and kept him company for three miles yesterday as he walked into the town of Cimarron. We had to load Stan into our car and search for his owner which we found thanks to the dog's excitement when we drove by the property. We were able to pray with the owner, a sweet Mexican woman. We're not sure she understood everything we were praying, but no doubt she felt our genuineness and sincerity.

We have been in the city of Dodge this week, a western town plagued by gangs and lawlessness a few years ago. Last weekend eighty cars and homes had their windows smashed by the rowdy element still lurking in the area. We are reminded daily that we need the protection of the Lord, and the scripture in Romans 5:20, "Where sin abounds, grace does much more abound," rings true no matter where we find ourselves.

This town is filled with rich western history, which we experienced firsthand when we visited the Santa Fe Trail Tracks area, a preserved section of prairie where you can see original wheel ruts from the thousands of wagons that passed through this area in the 1800's. We felt as if we stepped back into the pioneer days as we pictured the dust-covered, weary travelers who journeyed further west seeking a future filled with opportunity and prosperity.

Today we visited Boot Hill Museum, where thousands of artifacts from 150 years ago are preserved in a recreated wild western Main Street. Unfortunately, we missed the daily gun fight reenactment that begins Memorial Day. There is a strong Mexican flavor to this western town, with Mexican restaurants and businesses everywhere. We are enjoying the hilly terrain in this area, preparing ourselves for the changing, flat landscape that will be sure to surround us as we travel southwest. There is a very real possibility that some good friends of ours will travel from Texas to join us Tuesday and Wednesday. It will be refreshing to see some familiar faces and fellowship with some dear friends!

This week marked the halfway point of our planned six-month trip as well as the halfway mark for this leg. We continue to stand fast in the knowledge that God holds the future of our nation in His hands, and we just need to come alongside His will and agree with Him. May you also be assured that your future is lovingly gift wrapped by your loving Heavenly Father and waiting for you to open it and walk it out!

This faithful little fellow followed Calvin for three miles one day when he walked west from Dodge City, Kansas. We had to drive around until we found his owner.

This is the sign that greeted us as we entered Dodge City, Kansas.

These Kansas "skyscrapers" can be seen everywhere across the state and hold millions of pounds of grain.

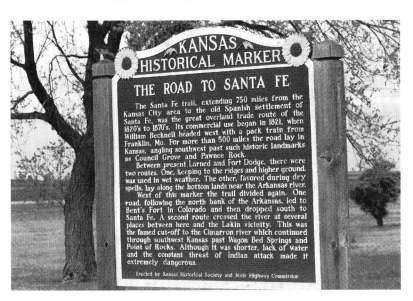

The Santa Fe Trail runs 750 miles from Kansas City to Santa Fe, New Mexico.

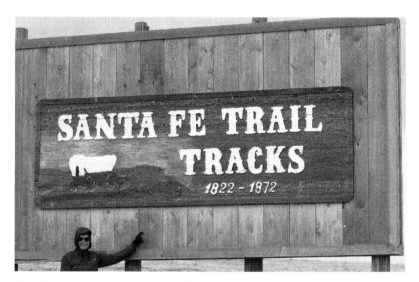

The day we arrived in Dodge City we traveled a short distance west of the city to see the preserved Santa Fe Trail Tracks.

On this morning, Calvin walked to the town of Cimarron. His road dead-ended and he ended up walking through the prairie, across a large field of wheat and on the Arkansas River bed. No he didn't walk on water; the river has been dried up for over twenty years.

Tumble weed could be found everywhere we went. These prairie bushes would blow across the road and pile up everywhere they could.

These beautiful animals covered the plains by the millions in the 1800's. By 1878, they had been over-hunted to the point of near extinction. Today they are raised on special ranches. This fellow is a resident at the Wright Park Zoo in Dodge City.

We spent Saturday afternoon exploring Boot Hill Museum and Historic District in Dodge City. This was the original jail they used in the 1870's to "cool down" the cowboy hot heads.

This is an actual photograph of a mountain of buffalo skulls and gives you an idea of the slaughter of buffalos that took place out west in the last half of the 1800's.

Igniting Destinies
May 8, 2014

We closed out last week with a God-ordained visit to Abundant Life Family Church. We got the connection from two girls we met the day before at the Dodge City Visitor's Center. (We spent the day Saturday exploring Boot Hill Museum, Fort Dodge and the surrounding areas). A guest speaker from Oklahoma was sharing Sunday morning, and we felt impressed to release the Oklahoma shepherd's staff to him to take along back to his state. We are trusting the staff will end up at the destination of God's choosing and will be instrumental in furthering God's purposes in the Sooner State, referring to the non-Native settlers who arrived in the state in the early 1900's.

Our adventures continued this week from our "home base" in Liberal, Kansas. This is the home of Dorothy Gale, the famous character in L. Frank Baum's book "The Wizard of Oz." Everywhere you go in town, the theme follows you, as bronze statues of Dorothy pepper the street corners. Hotels are everywhere since travelers come from far and wide to attend the International Pancake Day, The Land of Oz and Coronado Museum as well as the Mid-American Air Museum. Our dear friends, Chad and Shannon, made the trek from Fort Worth, Texas to visit us for a few days this week. What a wonderful time we had reconnecting and sharing the realities of our life on the road. We sent the Texas shepherd's staff along back with them to be given to one of two ministries in the Fort Worth area.

This week also presented us with some challenges since our map book is incomplete and leaves out many road names. When you see the geography of the region you can see why. The publishers probably never dreamed that someone would be traversing this wild, desert-like region on foot! We have found a mix of friends and foes in this region, and Calvin is anxious to continue his walk west. If he would walk due south, he would arrive in Oklahoma in a hour or two, but we are headed southwest to the panhandle of Oklahoma, referred to on the Oklahoma map as "No Man's Land." I'm sure we will get a greater revelation of what that means when we arrive there on Monday.

Messages, emails and phone calls we receive feel like lifelines from those we love back home. Calvin wanted to share one significant text he received this week, which is helping to carry him through some of the opposition he has faced recently:

"Your latter and your ladder will be greater! The prayers are ascending up the ladder. The answers are descending upon you—provision, dreams, vision, wisdom and love. You are speaking in the tongues of angels and they are responding to the words of the Lord within your heavenly language. Your ladder has gone into a higher place in the throne room—a spirit of counsel in the council room of the judge. Righteous decrees will flow from your lips like honey, full of mercy to cover and recover God's original intentions. Your latter will be greater! Greater glory is coming because you have suffered greater. Those who suffer must be glorified! You are on a trail of transfiguration! And it will alter you to set up altars like Abraham did along the way. Wells will spring up and mantels will be accumulated for the days to come. You have prepared the way and the Way has prepared you for more!

You are not going to the right or to the left but upward from glory to glory. Your ladder and your latter are greater!"

The further west we go, the more we realize that this country prospered and expanded on the backs of many innocent victims, the least of which were the native inhabitants. An "ingenious" strategy was used to literally push the Native Americans out of their homeland. Because the buffalo was their sole source of food, clothing, and shelter, the expansionists knew if they annihilated the buffalo, it would eliminate the Native Americans. It worked. By 1880, there were only a few thousand buffalo left to roam the open plains. The Natives were defeated with one fell swoop.

How far will we go to get ahead, to ensure our destiny will be realized? How many people do we leave in the wake of our human ambition? Our prayer is that many people will be blessed and true destinies ignited in the wake of the Spirit that we leave behind us as we travel onward. May you leave a trail of sweet smelling savor behind you as you serve Him this week. . . .

We were thrilled to present the Oklahoma shepherd's staff to Billy Dougoud who is from Tulsa, Oklahoma. Some new friends were made at Abundant Life Family Church, pastored by Jim and Lydia Ames. We were treated to lunch by some new friends we met there.

We spent Sunday morning fellowshipping in this wonderful church, Abundant Life Family Church in Dodge City, Kansas.

As we drove to Liberal, we came upon these beautiful, unexpected rolling dirt bluffs and canyons. What a nice change after weeks of endless flat plains.

Chad and Shannon Jennings made the eight-hour trip up to Liberal to visit with and encourage us. They are carrying the Texas shepherd's staff back with them to Fort Worth, Texas to be given to one of several ministries in their area. We loved spending time with and fellowshipping with these dear friends.

This map shows the original inhabitants of our country and their original homelands. Amazingly, most of these tribes were "relocated" to a few western states, and forced into reservations or colonies.

Calvin gave Chad, our friend from Texas, a crash course on walking gravel roads. They spent Wednesday morning prayer walking into Liberal, Kansas.

No Man's Land
May 16, 2014

Yesterday we arrived in New Mexico after a whirlwind stop in Oklahoma. Our stay in Boise City, Oklahoma (in the territory known as No Man's Land) showed us again how many of these remote areas are declining, both in population as well as economics. Boise City, population one thousand, is the county seat for Cimarron County. We visited Kenton, the northwestern-most town in Oklahoma, where a mere twenty people live without a bank, grocery store or gas station. Kenton sits along the beautiful Black Mesa, a welcome geological sight after four weeks of flat, endless Kansas prairie. During Calvin's few days of walking in this area, he met a wonderful Kenton local, Vicki, a strong believer who runs a beautiful Bed and Breakfast on a 1,200 acre ranch outside Kenton. Calvin felt led to give her his cedar shepherd's staff and to thank her for her faithfulness in blessing ministers and missionaries at her establishment in the rugged Black Mesa Hills.

Just a few miles northwest, we visited the three corners marker, where Oklahoma, Colorado and New Mexico meet. We spent some time praying that God's will would be accomplished in the tri-state area—this land that was birthed through the strong pioneer spirit. At the end of a gravel lane, we stood in the same place where dinosaurs roamed so long ago and we gazed in amazement at the footprints they left behind. The Black Mesa area is home to two "Dinosaur bone quarries," where years before, hundreds of dinosaur bones were excavated.

We were also blessed by the hospitality of the director and volunteers at the Cimarron County Heritage Center who gave us a special tour covering the 107-year history, from the days of the Dust Bowl, through the unfortunate bombing during World War II, until present day. As it is everywhere we visit, the residents are profoundly proud of their local heritage, which is colored by the history of the Santa Fe Trail, and many years of the cattle industry, and their history of local track and field champions.

En route to Clayton, New Mexico, we traveled the Dry Cimarron Scenic Byway, where thousands-year-old rock formations greeted us as we wound our way along the red gravel road. We drove the harrowing road to the top of Capulin Volcano, an extinct cinder cone volcano, which rises thirteen hundred feet above the plains. Calvin hiked the Crater Rim Trail, rising 8,182 feet above sea level, and prayed for the three states that are visible from the top. How mysterious and captivating is this barren 8,000 square mile Rayton-Clayton volcanic field, dotted with extinct volcanos and lava-capped mesas. The firmament does indeed display His handi-work! (See Psalm 19:1 and Romans 1:20).

In ten days we will be walking once again upon our own familiar land back in Pennsylvania, reuniting with family, friends and our pets. Today, God reminded us that it is important that we stay focused on the task at hand and that we finish the work well. Living day by day in His presence and provision is one way we can accomplish this. This week when we met Anne, a Catholic pilgrim, who is walking along the Santa Fe Trail from Missouri to Santa Fe, New Mexico, we were challenged by our lack of faith. She carries only a backpack with a few clothes, a cross and a book. No cell phone, no GPS, no money, and no food—only her faith that each day she will be given what she needs. She sleeps at local churches and farmhouses along the way, asking for nothing but a sofa to sleep on and a plate of food. During the past seven years she has traversed South and Central America, Europe and across Africa to Jerusalem. Would we be willing to live that kind of radical faith if God asked us? Where has the spirit of the first-century church gone? Has it been swallowed up by our reliance on technology, by our self-sufficient independence and endless plans and administrations? May we all, like Anne, be ready to say, "Here I am Lord, send me. . . ."

This beautiful stone sign greeted us as we drove across the state line from Kansas. After four weeks in Kansas, this was a welcome sight. Just imagine how the pioneers felt!

Many of the rock formations have been given names. We could sit and gaze at these incredible formations for hours.

On the way to Black Mesa State Park, we saw this dinosaur femur bone at a dinosaur dig site. It's amazing to think these majestic creatures trod on the same soil eons ago.

This outcropping of stones is called the Wedding Party (the minister is in the foreground with the bride and groom next and the wedding guests behind).

Calvin walks many hours in the remote parts of the region we are in. He can stay focused on prayer, not having to worry about traffic and other distractions.

We found ourselves just a mile from the Texas border at the end of one of Calvin's walks, so we drove over the border to say hi!

Everywhere we go we are surrounded by mountains of tumble weed. If it could nest in our hair, I think it would.

Patriotism was on
display everywhere we
journeyed.

*We had no idea that this
part of the country is
famous for their dinosaur
excavation sites. We
were awed by the well-
preserved tracks we
found back a farmer's
lane just south of Three
Corners.*

We drove back from the Three Corners just in time to catch Vicki leaving for her mail route. She was thrilled to receive the cedar staff that Calvin gave her. He shared with her that it was a big thank you from the Lord for her heart to bless ministers and missionaries with complimentary time at their beautiful Bed & Breakfast.

We drove to the marker where Colorado, New Mexico and Oklahoma join. We spent some time praying over and anointing the area, trusting that God will move and bring revival to this area of the country.

Praying for the tri-state area.

As we drove through the north east corner of Oklahoma, these unique rock formations popped up around every corner. I felt like my soul came alive after four weeks of flat, dry, windy prairies that were my only visual stimulation.

The beautiful, unique landscape of this mysterious land captivated us from the first day we entered this state.

This was my favorite rock formation. I made Calvin slam on the brakes many times so I could get pictures of these beautiful sights.

This was the view from the top of Capulin Volcano looking out across the Raton-Clayton volcano field.

Calvin walked around the rim of Capulin Volcano praying for the three states that could be seen off in the distance.

We came upon these white-tailed deer calmly grazing beside the road. I was able to capture them as they leapt over the fence into safer pasture.

On our way to Clayton we drove to Capulin Volcano, an extinct cone volcano which sits in the 8,000 square mile Rayton-Clayton volcano field.

Creepy, Crawly, Slithering Things

Calvin has become a herpe-tologist of sorts in the last four years. Who else do you know that houses twenty turtles in a backyard turtle garden? I affectionately refer to this area of the yard as the "Turtle Resort" and tease him that his turtles live a better life than many homeless

individuals. After all, they are surrounded by luxurious sand, beautiful foliage and even their own strawberries. It is with this mentality that Calvin entered into the southwest leg of our cross country walk. Anything that slithered or crawled was cause to pause, investigate and admire. Some days lizards were his only companions—you won't find too many living creatures thriving in desert environments.

Calvin's first snake sighting occurred along the Flint Hills Trail deep in the flatland of Kansas. It was merely a long, narrow green snake that stretched four to five feet across the rock-strewn trail. Being the lover of nature that he is, Calvin gingerly picked up the snake to examine it closer. Only when it began to curl and writhe did he drop it at the side of the trail and watch it hurry off into the dust.

The second sighting happened as Calvin plodded along one of the many gravel roads that predictably ran north and south and east and west across the entire state of Kansas with grid-like precision. Curled at the side of the road, basking in the warm spring sun, was a tan snake with black markings. Calvin wasn't a snake expert, but to him it sure looked like a rattlesnake. He resisted the urge to get closer, but instead documented his new find by taking several pictures so he could research the species later. Our on-line search to reveal the creature's identity proved fruitless. Several days later, Calvin met and befriended a local farmer who was bustling about his work on his thousands-acre spread. After describing the snake to his new friend, Calvin discovered with disappointment that it was merely a bull snake, a species that is evidently quite common in Kansas. The farmers even used them as a kind of nature-made barometer—when a bull snake is seen crossing the road, it is a sure sign of rain. The farmer's guess was that most of the local bull snakes had gotten used to a one-sided existence as the state was in the midst of a five-year drought with no sign of rain in the near future.

A few weeks later, our wanderings took us to Black Mesa State Park in the far northwest corner of Oklahoma's panhandle. The majestic rock outcroppings were a stunning sight after four weeks of flat, open prairie. A beautiful lake lay nestled in a valley. Colorful rock formations hovered over the dark water that waited patiently for the summer anglers to rustle it awake. As we drove slowly away from the park, we passed cattle roaming freely back and forth across the open road. A large, dark raven dove suddenly to our left and wrestled with something in the grass. To our amazement, the raven emerged with a long, dark creature struggling to break free from its determined captor. Off into the cloud-filled sky they flew, the raven and his snake, a poignant picture of the struggle for survival here in the untamed wilderness.

Feeling confident that his snake identification skills were growing now, Calvin was not surprised when he spotted three snakes along a remote back road in the wilderness of Clayton, New Mexico. After studying the road map for an appropriate road to walk that day, he had discovered there was literally only one back road in the area. A New Mexican back road is an authentic "back" road where cattle roam unhindered by fence or rail, and the only humans passing through are the occasional ranchers driving their pick-up trucks to some remote field. Calvin must have been a curious sight for those docile beasts as they rambled up to examine the strange human who tramped where only beasts and reptiles dared to tread.

The western rattlesnake and the bull snake share similar patterns and are sometimes mistaken for each other. The first snake Calvin saw that morning lay coiled and seemingly asleep alongside the dirt road. "Just another bull snake," he muttered and stepped closer to take a few pictures. He instinctively jumped back as he spotted the unmistakable rattle at the end of his long, sleek body. Calvin quickly snapped a few more pictures before moving on to safer ground. "That was no bull snake!" The reality that he was out on a remote back road with most likely no cell phone reception crept into his mind that was now vigilant and fully awake. Getting a few good pictures was not worth the risk of a potentially life-threatening snack bite in the middle of the New Mexico wilderness.

Calvin came upon two more bull snakes that day, one of which had mysteriously disappeared by the time he was picked up at the end of the day. But it seemed his snake sightings were destined to continue. During our short stay in Santa Fe, New

Mexico, Calvin visited a pet store located along one of the main streets of the city. It was his kind of store—reptiles, snakes, and other assorted creatures filled the place with screeching and rustlings of every sort. Calvin knew he couldn't purchase any to take along home, but he could immerse himself in the beauty of life all around, something he missed as he traversed the desolate wilderness of the southwest with its few animal residents. Suddenly, the owner yelled from the across the room.

"Hey you, you better watch out!" His eyes widened as he looked above Calvin's head.

"What in the world? What could he be worked up about?" Calvin asked as he tentatively looked up towards the ceiling. There, in all its massive beauty, slithering silently towards Calvin's unsuspecting head was one of the largest Boa Constrictors

Calvin had ever seen. The snake was winding down from his wooden perch that was wired into the ceiling, stretching ever further towards his prey. It seemed that Calvin could not escape these amazing creatures—but he could choose to keep a safe distance!

This harmless green snake wound its way across Calvin's path on the Flint Hills Nature Trail.

Calvin is always watching for snakes as he walks. Although these are harmless, they are quite an ominous sight. We were told that rattle snakes don't live at these altitudes here in Santa Fe, so Calvin has had a break from his daily vigil.

Only after Calvin snapped a few close-up pictures did he realize this was the real thing—a western rattlesnake!

Sowing Seeds in the Southwest
May 23, 2014

We are wrapping up the last week of this leg of our journey in the high desert city of Santa Fe, New Mexico. Here at 7,100 feet elevation we are bordered by the majestic mountains of the Jemez range to the northwest and the Sangre de Christo to the northeast. Snow-capped peaks winked their welcome as we drove into the city following the famous Santa Fe Trail. Thanks to a city code that was passed in 1912, adobe homes and businesses dressed in shades of tan, sienna and brown pepper the hillsides. The architectural flavor of the city blends with the earth and one feels transported back through the centuries to when the Spanish first settled the area four hundred years ago.

The city boasts our nation's oldest house and the oldest functioning church, San Miguel Mission Church, built in 1610. Santa Fe is an artist's paradise, with galleries showcasing their talents throughout the city. In the downtown district we were excited to visit Loretta Chapel, built in 1873, and home to the "miraculous staircase." Legend has it that when the chapel was complete, the Sisters realized that a traditional staircase to the choir loft would be impossible since it would take up too much of the sanctuary space. After nine days of prayer, an unknown carpenter appeared at the chapel door, riding on a donkey and carrying only a small tool kit. In six months, he constructed a spiral staircase that has two 360 degree turns and no visible means of support. After completing this engineering feat, he simply vanished and was never heard from again.

Calvin has been taking advantage of the many trails that traverse the city and surrounding countryside. The skirting lizards, curious prairie dogs and the cloud-dotted sky are Calvin's only companions as he plods along the dusty trails that taste rain a mere fifty days a year. He made the trek south to Eldorado one day; another day he started north of the city and walked the sidewalks through town and back to our hotel.

There is a strong Catholic, Spanish and Native American presence here and once again we have felt at a disadvantage, not knowing Spanish. As always, we have met fellow believers here who are following Christ, living a godly life, and making a difference in their own sphere of influence.

With almost four months of The National Cross Walk behind us, questions linger and emotions rise to the surface. Are we being effective? Are we making a difference through our prayers and by our presence in each area? Much of what we do is to throw seeds into fertile ground and trust God to bring a supernatural multiplication as they germinate, spring up and finally bear fruit. How can we measure naturally what God is doing in the Spirit?

On May 27 we will arrive home to another world—one filled with reuniting with family and friends, caring for loved ones, sorting through two months of mail, and accomplishing necessary work. We ask that you continue in prayer for us—without it we know we cannot go forward in what God has asked us to do. Your generous financial support will enable us to begin the next and final leg of this epic journey and to ultimately complete the assignment the Lord has entrusted us with. We look forward to connecting with you again by email in the middle of June when we will be back out on the road. In the meantime, we would love to hear from you while we are home on break in Pennsylvania from May 27-June 10!

Calvin walked seventeen miles on this lonely gravel road west of Clayton. He saw his first official rattlesnake that day as well as two bull snakes. There were no fences to keep the cattle in, and at one point he was surrounded by these curious creatures. No doubt Calvin broke the monotony of their day, and they certainly gave him some excitement!

The cattle are left to roam freely through fields and across roads- it seems they have the right-of-way.

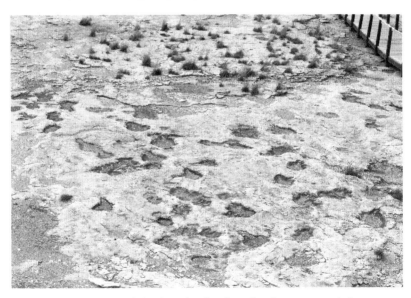

Here is an example of the hundreds of perfectly preserved dinosaur tracks. The tracks were discovered when they built the dam behind the Clayton Lake.

These amazing relics are the only things that remain of Fort Union, the largest U.S. military installation on the 1800's southwest frontier. It was a remote garrison that was in use from 1851-1891. Many locals pilfered the remaining walls and stones until the National Park Service began its stewardship of the site in the 1950's.

Everywhere we go we find patriotic spirit in our country. As you can see in this picture, the wind didn't stay in Kansas!

San Miguel Mission Church- This beautiful adobe church is the oldest functioning church in the United States. It was built in 1610 when the area was Spanish ruled.

Beside the San Miguel Mission Church stands the oldest existing house in the United States, built in 1646.

Calvin began his week of walking in Santa Fe at the Rail Yard in the city. Many trails wind their way throughout the city and out into the surrounding area.

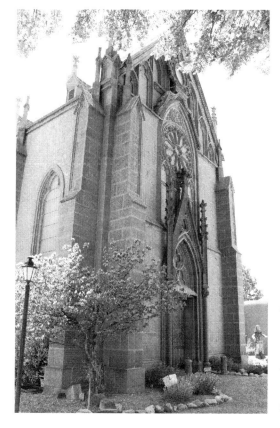

We couldn't leave Santa Fe without visiting the "miraculous" staircase at Loretta Chapel, built in 1873. The chapel is still in use for concerts, weddings and special occasions.

The craftsmanship of this staircase is breathtaking. The unknown carpenter used only a hammer, a saw, water, and a carpenter's square to complete the job. It took him six months and he left before the Sisters had the chance to pay him. Engineers are still baffled by the fact that it had no side supports.

These adorable little creatures were all over the field at Frenchy's Field, an area that Calvin passed several times. They were quite sociable and would pop up out of their holes, stare at us, and chatter away as we walked by.

Calvin walked the La Tierra Trail north of the city to downtown Santa Fe. He walked around the capital declaring God's reign in the city.

A "Typical" Day on the Road
June 13, 2014

Here we are back on the road after a fleeting two week "break" back home in Pennsylvania. Many of you have asked what a typical day is like for us, so I thought I'd give you a glimpse into what our lives have been like over the past four months. And for those of you who have worried that I'm languishing in boredom, this is my opportunity to put your fears to rest!

Our day begins with either the slamming of doors from other not-so-sensitive hotel guests, or with the first rays of the relentless desert sun. I jump start each day either in the fitness room, the hotel pool or at a nearby park, where I exercise and brush off the cobwebs of the hopefully sound night's sleep. Calvin showers, eats a light breakfast, prepares his day's rations and water supply and applies copious sun screen for the day's walk. If I'm staying out on the road, I take a quick shower, prepare my breakfast on the one-burner stove in our room while watching the Weather Channel for any severe weather updates, and pack food and reading material for the day. We double check our gear, make sure we have our map book and GPS and hit the road anywhere between eight and nine a.m. If the road where Calvin plans to walk is secure, I do a drop off at his starting point. We pray over the day, go over our emergency back-up plan, and take pictures and footage of what Calvin feels the Lord has given him to pray for the day. I then return to the hotel room to tackle my to-do list and wait for regular updates from Calvin during the day. We stay in constant contact and I need to be ready to leave within minutes if he encounters a problem on the road or if the weather turns. Here in the southwest, the danger of heat stroke or dehydration, due to the extreme heat, is always on our minds. Because we are still at 4,500 feet elevation here in Socorro, our breathing, sleeping and energy levels are still affected. We drink twice the water we normally would to ward off headaches and fatigue. One of Calvin's biggest concerns is running out of water while out on the road.

Calvin spends most of his time in prayer for the region as well as whatever the Lord puts on his heart as he traverses the desolate countryside, back-dropped by the Chupadera Mountains. He makes and receives phone calls while he's out on the road and stops to talk to anyone he sees outside or who stops to offer him a ride. God has opened up lots of opportunities for Calvin to share about our walk, ask questions about the local area, and encourage and pray for the new "friends" he meets on the road. He always has his small camera handy, ready to document his day.

My days are filled with endless emails, website updates, phone calls, laundry visits, food runs, studying, writing, and planning for the days ahead. Hotel reservations need to be made in advance and correspondence with family and friends always depends on the internet connection in each local area.

Monday we will arrive in Arizona and continue on into the curious mix of towering national forests and stark desert beauty. Lizards, jack rabbits, snakes and road runners will be Calvin's only travel mates as he journeys on towards the western shore. Are there days when we wonder if it's all worth it? Of course ...

but we plod on knowing that the prayers of a righteous man are effective! Yesterday God gave Calvin five themes to pray about and declare: Conviction, revelation, visions, dreams and salvation (Acts 2 and Joel 2). The need for these to become a reality rings in our spirits as we hear how the local youth are plagued by drug abuse and apathy. There is an average of three drug overdoses a month here in this small city of nine thousand people. The city was named "Socorro," which means "aid," in reference to 1598, when the Piro Indians gave food to Spanish settlers who had crossed an uninhabitable stretch of desert in southern New Mexico. In the same way, we believe God sent us to Socorro to aid the people here, to blaze a trail in the Spirit from which this conviction, revelation, visions, dreams and salvation may flow. Please agree with us that God's presence will flood this parched region here in southwest New Mexico and that the purposes and destiny of God will reign!

Land of Contradictions
June 18, 2014

As I write this I am sitting at Woodland Park in the beautiful mountain town of Pinetop-Lakeside, Arizona. This state is indeed a land of contradictions. We just spent three days in the town of Springerville, a valley town surrounded by the White Mountains, many which shine tan and barren in the western setting sun. Just north of us lies the Petrified Forest, where the desert floor is scattered with stone-like wood from millennia gone by. We are now surrounded by tall pines and lakes sprinkled across this mountain resort area that sits on the edge of Fort Apache Indian Reservation and the Apache Sitgreaves National Forest. Two thousand different varieties of cacti, twenty distinct Indian nations, and the majestic Grand Canyon are just a few of the fascinating home-grown attractions that draw thousands of visitors here each year. We've been enjoying the high desert altitudes above seven thousand feet where the air is cool and dry, and the wind sweeps across the varied landscape that is peppered with ancient extinct volcanoes and towering Alpine-covered peaks. In one week we will be entering the oven-hot Phoenix area where the average temperature is 105 degrees this time of year.

Rain is a scarce and coveted commodity here in the southwest. Calvin has been diligent in praying for the much needed rain, and we were thrilled to hear that the southwest part of Kansas received three inches of rain while we were home on break. That is the exact amount Calvin had been petitioning the Lord for the last few weeks we were trudging through that sunbaked state. Keith from Elkhart, Kansas, whom we met at our hotel, excitedly shared with us that on June 5 and 6, they welcomed two days of much needed rain equaling three inches! In Socorro, where Calvin presented a walking stick to the leadership of the Potter's House Church, we were pleasantly surprised by a full hour of steady rain one afternoon, a rare occurrence according to the locals there. Calvin was forced to dart into a Walmart to wait out the storm, and was amused by the exclamations of the shoppers whom he overheard saying, "This never happens in Socorro!" We even found out later through an email from a supporter that the rain in the Socorro area usually evaporates before it even hits the ground. We serve an amazing God!

We ended our time in Springerville with Calvin presenting a pine tree to Pastor Dennis, senior pastor of the First Assembly of God Church. The church is located in a complex that spans two and one-half city blocks on the east end of town. The tree represents Isaiah 60:13 and Isaiah 41:17-20, where the pine tree signifies life in the desert and beauty and fragrance all year long. Calvin saw the tree as a visual reminder to the church of the tenderness of the youth in the community and how they need the same tender loving care as that young pine tree. Springerville has seen an unprecedented number of suicides this past year, a fact which lies heavy on the heart of the churches there in town. First Assembly is a shining beacon to the community, housing a women's ministry, where pregnancy testing and counseling takes place, as well as parenting and financial stewardship classes. The church also boasts a bus ministry to the unchurched children from town and a children's enrichment program. Pastor Dennis leads a county-wide food pantry program that provides much needed sustenance to those facing financial hardships throughout Apache County.

In just four short weeks, we will be standing in the waters of the Pacific Ocean, marking the end of our cross country prayer walk. We can only imagine what God has accomplished through this season of faith, endurance and love—love for God and for this great country of ours. Recently, Calvin has been stirred each time he sees the American flag, the symbol of our great nation. He sees this as a constant confirmation that God is the author and finisher of our prayer walk, and we leave the results up to Him. We will soon be celebrating the anniversary of our country's hard-fought independence. While you are celebrating, remember to thank God for the freedoms you enjoy each and every day and say a prayer that the destiny and future of our nation will be dedicated to the will of God Almighty!

We spent a few hours Wednesday morning walking the cliffs examining the 400-700 year old images which were etched into the black desert stones by ancestors of today's Native people.

The town of Socorro dates back to 1598.

Calvin is sun-screened up and ready to walk from Socorro, New Mexico going west on Route 60. Our third and final leg has begun! The forecast is ninety degrees plus well into next week. Monday we will cross the border into Arizona!

Although most rain evaporates before it hits the ground in this area, we were blessed with almost an hour of heavy rain the first day Calvin walked in this desert New Mexico town.

Calvin walked through the White Mountains from Socorro to Magdalena. The temperature was comfortable but the winds whipped across the barren landscape which brought back memories of Kansas.

Calvin and I are always up for a little extra adventure, so we couldn't resist this sign pointing the way to the Ghost Town of Kelly, New Mexico.

Kelly was once a bustling town of 3,000 back in the 1800's when it was in its peak silver and zinc mining era. In 2012 it was re-established and consists of one dwelling and one church. No utilities are available, so they're on their own.

What was once a thriving mining town has now been reduced to deteriorating walls and foundations and the rusting silence of mining equipment.

We could never get over the majesty of Magdalena Peak right outside of our hotel window. It continued to awe us the entire time we stayed in Socorro. What this area lacks in plants and trees it makes up for in mountain magic...

This brother shared with us how God answered our specific prayer for three inches of rain in southwest Kansas. He was more excited than we were since they have been in a severe drought for five years.

We crossed over the Continental Divide on our way to Springerville, Arizona.

We stopped at this amazing place on our way to Springerville, Arizona. It is one of the most extensive radio telescope sites in the world and uses cutting edge technology to study the vast reaches of the universe.

There are 28 of these massive one hundred ton discs that work in harmony to receive radio light waves. These are then interpreted into pictures of the far reaches of the heavens.

The sun sets early here in the South West - around 7:30 p.m. Calvin can't pass up the chance to photograph yet one more sun set in the high desert.

Calvin felt led to present this pine tree to Pastor Dennis. It represents the need to love and nurture the youth of the Springerville area. There have been six suicides just this year in this small town of 6,000.

We drove through this beautiful reservation land on our way to Pinetop-Lakeside, Arizona.

Calvin enjoyed walking in the resort town of Pinetop, where he was surrounded by towering Aspen Pines.

Connections
June 25, 2014

Connection, connection, connection! This has been the emphasis of the third leg of the National Cross Walk so far. The natural beauty of the Pinetop-Lakeside area was enunciated by the inspiring believers we met during our short time there. Ernie pastors "The Church" in Pinetop. They have an active youth ministry and outreach to the Apache Youth on the Res (short for Reservation). Calvin released a shepherd's staff to them to signify their influence in the community. Evangeline, an Apache Christian, spent time praying with Calvin for the salvation of her people. She teaches the children in her community, and so Calvin presented her with a small shepherd's staff to signify her position of authority among her people. Our hearts broke as she shared with us the great needs in her hometown of Cibecue, Arizona. Driving through the vast wilderness of the White Mountains, we wonder how these strong, resilient people have made a life for themselves here. Native artisans keep the art of their culture alive, showcasing their handiwork at various craft shows and festivals. Casinos dot the parched landscape throughout the state, which brings in much needed revenue for the Native American peoples. We listen attentively in public places where families converse in their native tongues. Such diversity in this vast nation of ours!

Sunday morning we found ourselves at New Living Church in Lakeside, Arizona, pastored by Richard and Patricia Boen. His message on preparation for the last days encouraged and challenged us. After the service we met with Evangeline, our new Apache friend, and prayed for her, her daughter, Katie, and for an outpouring of God's Spirit among her people.

Driving to Globe, we wove our way through the endless White Mountains, passing through Salt River Canyon, the area's "Little Grand Canyon." As we navigated the hairpin turns, we passed many southerners making their way from the scorching valley up into the refreshing mountain resort towns. We wound down the mountain and watched the thermometer creep ever closer to the century mark. We will have to get used to this oppressive heat over the next few weeks—a heat that saps the very essence of life from your body. Calvin has found that by drinking a continual flow of water throughout the day he can ward off dehydration that constantly threatens in this excessive heat.

In Globe, Calvin connected with two Assembly of God pastors, John and Allen, who both prayed with him for revival in this area and beyond, unity among the churches, the need for godly leadership, and a passion to reach the lost. This area has rich deposits of gold and copper, which are mined here, and then portions are transported to Mexico and shipped on to China. We pray that along with these abundant natural resources, this area would be known as a strategic center of revival.

Today, we arrived in the greater Phoenix area, which has grown to a population of three million since World War II. We toured the Superstition Mountain Museum, where we were told that Phoenix has over one hundred days of more than 100-degree weather. We believed them when our car thermometer hit 108 on the way to our hotel! Searching for shade will be my primary responsibility over the next week.

Calvin looks forward to covering much of the Greater Phoenix area throughout the week ahead. He will be starting out early each day and walk until the sun and oppressive heat make it unsafe to continue. We long for the green of home, but are fascinated by the towering Saguaro cacti that are sprinkled across the barren mountains, stretching out their arms in greeting throughout southern Arizona.

Please remember to lift us up in prayer over the next two weeks, as we will be battling the elements once again—this time heat and sun.

These are a few of the wonderful believers we met at The New Living Church in Lakeside, Arizona. The beautiful eagle is hand painted on their foyer wall.

"Pastor Ernie shepherds The Church and has an active ministry to The Apache people. Calvin presented him with a shepherd's staff to signify his authority in this region in Arizona."

Here are a few of the amazing young men from The Church Youth Group.

Everywhere we go there is a constant threat of forest fires. This one was burning not far from the Apache town of Cibecue. The monsoon season starts in a few weeks. It will rain every day but only last for a month.

We prayed with our new friends, Evangeline and Katie, and gave them a child-sized shepherd's staff for their work with the children of their community. What sweet spirits!

On this particular day, Calvin began walking east of Globe, in the town of Cutter, inside the Fort Apache Reservation. Because of the increasing heat, he sometimes carries a gallon of water and bottles of ice water and Gatorade in his sling. He has received lots of warnings from people about the dangers of dehydration.

Scott and Rocky drive twelve hour shifts hauling raw materials to the gold and copper mines in Globe.

Without clouds to paint the sky, this is what a desert sunset looks like. Our sunset here arrives around 7:30 p.m. verses the later Pennsylvania sunset.

We had some glorious sights driving through the "Little Grand Canyon" down into the valley towards Globe, Arizona.

These majestic cacti are found everywhere. Normally their spiny arms stretch straight out, but once in a while their arms wrap around in a "hug."

The Heat is On!
July 1, 2014

In a few days, Calvin will finish his prayer walking in the Phoenix area. According to the locals, we have had a "cooler" summer so far (I never thought of 106-112 degrees as being in the "cooler" range, but this trip has presented us with many firsts). The only wildlife that seems to thrive in this hot, arid climate is lizards, road runners and different species of ants. The skies sport azure blue each day with no sign of the monsoon rains that are due to arrive within the next two weeks.

We awoke one morning last week to the report of a 5.6 magnitude earthquake that rattled the town of Safford, Arizona, about 130 miles southeast of Phoenix. We were asleep when it happened, so we had no idea that it was felt in our area. Since earthquakes are not prone to shake the Grand Canyon State, some Arizonans' nerves were shaken along with the pictures on the walls.

Calvin continues to connect with local churches and is blessed by their hearts to reach this area where 4.3 million people reside, the thirteenth largest metropolitan area in the nation. During one day of walking west through Mesa, he met Joni, Ed and Pastor Greg at City of Grace Church. They agreed together for a move of God in this strategic city. On another day, while walking north into Scottsdale, he prayed with John, Allen and Chris at Rock Church. On Sunday, we attended Living Word Bible Church in Mesa, where we presented the Arizona shepherd's staff to Dr. Tom and Maureen Anderson, senior pastors of this influential ministry. They oversee three other churches in the area and 32 churches across the nation. What a precious time of prayer and encouragement we had with them between two of the four services they hold there on Sundays.

Monday, Calvin walked throughout the downtown area, and was struck by the number of homeless individuals sitting in the intense heat. Bill and Martin were among those he talked to, and Calvin was delighted to lead Martin in the sinner's prayer. The Salvation Army ministry is visible in the city, where Calvin met Dana and Nanci, just a few of the hard working staff who labor to meet the spiritual and physical needs of those less fortunate in the city—a city surrounded on all sides by extreme affluence and the blessing of God. The evidence of the state's motto, Ditat Deus, "God enriches," is evident as we walk and drive through the prosperous neighborhoods bordering the downtown area. At the same time, strip clubs and nude bars line the main streets of the city. Even though prayer is the foundation for an outpouring of God's Spirit in this cosmopolitan area, God needs soldiers who are willing to go into the trenches where the hurting, needy people are. Wherever he goes, Calvin has begun to challenge the church leaders in the area to network together. Just think of what will be accomplished when we, as the body of Christ, surrender our own agendas and join forces to see the kingdom of darkness dethroned in our cities and towns across this nation? A house divided against itself cannot stand. Jesus' prayer that we would be one, even as He and His Father are one, rings in our hearts as we travel west.

For those of you who wonder what Calvin prays as he labors in prayer across our nation, here are some verses that he has been praying during our time in this area. Please agree with us as you continue to partner with us in prayer. Matthew 6:33; Luke 4:18-20; Luke 11:1-13; Luke 18:1-8; 1 Corinthians 15:10; Romans 5:1-5, 17; Matthew 10:16; Psalm 8:1-9; Psalm 84:11; Psalm 149.

In just sixteen days we will arrive at our final destination—the Pacific Ocean. Will you commit to stand with us until we arrive on that western shore?

Calvin began his walk in the Phoenix area in Apache Junction – an eastern suburb.

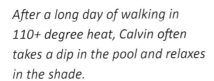

After a long day of walking in 110+ degree heat, Calvin often takes a dip in the pool and relaxes in the shade.

We drove up into the mountains to discover this beautiful pristine lake nestled between the mountain peaks.

This was a gorgeous oasis sitting above the steaming valley. Just the sight refreshed us.

Let it Rain
July 7, 2014

The night before we said our final farewell to the Phoenix area, we experienced the first rain storm of their monsoon season. It started off with a significant wind storm that Calvin watched blow up from the south. Then the rains began which brought everyone outside to watch. This was the first measureable rain the area received in 123 days and was a direct answer to Calvin's prayer that God would bring an outpouring of His Spirit, as well as the physical rain they so desperately need. What a refreshing way to end our week of extreme heat in this huge metropolitan area.

On July 4th we wound our way through the wilderness of western Arizona into the desert area of California. We drove just south of the Mojave Desert, with its fascinating dune formations and forbidding landscape. Signs of the severe drought that has plagued this area for the last few years were all around, as even the cacti seemed stunted and shriveled. The enormous Joshua Tree National Park, all 800,000 acres, bordered us to the north as we drove through mile after mile of desolation. As soon as we saw the hundreds of wind turbines in the distance we knew we were approaching the Coachella Valley, where a bundle of nine cities lie nestled between the Indio Hills on the northeast, standing in the shadow of the Little San Bernardino Mountains, with the San Jacinto Mountains to the southwest. San Jacinto Peak, the granddaddy of them all, looms tall and proud at 10, 804 feet at the edge of Palm Springs, our current base. This desert city, which boasts 350 days of sunshine a year, is a resort town, and the sight of many Hollywood films. After settling into our hotel, we toured the city and ended up watching the holiday fireworks that were set off from the downtown stadium.

Sunday we attended a small church in Cathedral City—Living Water Church of the Desert. We really appreciated their heart for prayer and evangelism and were warmly received. We feel so blessed to have seen so many expressions of the body of Christ across our nation. The same message is preached and embraced, with just the outward expressions being different and unique to the vision of the body there. We thought back to our early years as Christians, when we met in parks and homes with only a guitar and our voices for worship. Those were years of revival and radical commitment as young people were set free from years of addiction and pain. Our hearts yearn for this kind of hard-core revival to sweep our nation once more. God is looking for the hearts of His people to turn back to Him, forsaking the lure and trappings of the world. May the Lord retain this heart within us as we adjust back into life in Pennsylvania.

Calvin has three days to saturate this area in prayer and intercession. Some scriptures the Lord is impressing on him are Isaiah 6:1-3, Isaiah 40:1-5, Isaiah 60: 1-6, Numbers 14:21 and Habakkuk 2:14, which refer to the glory of the Lord covering the earth. Calvin's prayer is that we, as individuals and as a nation, would arise and shine for the glory of the Lord is rising upon us.

Please continue to pray for protection as the heat seems even more intense here since the humidity is a bit higher. Rain is never in the forecast with the temperatures reaching well over 110 degrees this time of year. Thursday we move on to Fontana,

California, a suburb of Los Angeles, where hopefully the climate will be a bit kinder. Please continue to pray and agree with us for a revelation of truth in the Los Angeles area, which is a hot bed of creativity but also humanistic thought. This is the seat of the entertainment world, which we believe will be saturated by the light of the gospel. The string of family-oriented, Christian-themed movies that came out this spring is an indication that God is indeed opening the doors in this influential, billion dollar industry.

Presenting the Arizona shepherd's staff to Dr. Tom and Maureen Anderson at Living Word Bible Church in Mesa, Arizona.

Many homes are built into the cliffs in the southwest. At least they don't have to worry about mowing the lawn...

Calvin was a trouper and walked in the extreme heat, no matter how hot it was. He often started in the early morning hours, even though it never dipped lower than the 90's at night. Our highest recorded temperature was 117 degrees!

Calvin was determined that we would see rain before we left the Phoenix area. The last night before we moved on, a "surprise" storm blew up.

The Arizona sky has a life all its own; it's full of vibrant colors that splash across the sky.

The surprise rain storm was preceded by a classic dust storm that we could watch blowing up from the south.

After 123 days with no rain, the Phoenix rain was a welcome sight. It brought many people out into the streets to enjoy it.

This was a typical sight in our hotel room each time we got ready to move on to our next "base camp."

Hundreds of wind turbines greeted us as we drove into the Coachella Valley on our way to Palm Springs, California.

Our first destination in California- Palm Springs. They enjoy an amazing 350 days of sunshine here at the edge of the Mojave Desert.

We attended Living Water Church of the Desert while we stayed in Palm Springs.

Hummingbird

These beautiful banners could be seen hanging from the light posts in Rancho Mirage, California.

We celebrated our country's Independence celebration at Central Park in downtown Palm Springs.

California Dreamin'
July 15, 2014

Driving into the greater Los Angeles area on our way to Fontana, California, we could sense the increase in the energy of the area along with the infamous Los Angeles traffic. Thousands of commuters clog the various freeways that weave in and out of this region, which houses eighteen million people and boasts the second largest metropolitan area of the country. To say that we, two country bumpkins from the farmlands of Lancaster County, are out of our comfort zones is an understatement. Negotiating the ten-lane highways takes all our concentration.

We had three productive days in San Bernardino and Fontana, California, located at the base of the "foothills" as the locals call them. It is a joy for Calvin to walk in the shadow of these majestic peaks, which keep him company as he pounds the endless sidewalks through city after city. He continues to connect with local churches. Set Free San Bernardino is one such church, which has a tremendous outreach in the city. Calvin was able to pray with Pastor Jeff and one of his intercessors Felepa—strangers, yet brothers and sister serving the same King, touching the heart of God, laboring in the same harvest field.

Saturday we drove up into the "Little" San Bernardino Mountains to Silverwood Lake to escape the relentless heat and suffocating smog intertwined with rising humidity. Many families from the valley go there to swim and boat in the mountain water. The "beaches" were nothing like the fine, white sand of Florida that I was used to, but it felt good to unwind and breathe the clearer air at six thousand feet above sea level. At the suggestion of a friend in Harrisburg, we attended San Bernardino Community Church on Sunday morning. Students from the Southern California Teen Challenge Centers sang and shared their testimonies. They showed us that even though we cry out for supernatural miracles as promised in the Bible, the greatest miracle is still that of God taking a selfish, evil heart controlled by Satan, and transforming it into a new heart surrendered to the Lord Jesus.

Monday, we moved further west, entering the official suburbs of Los Angeles. Our "base camp" is in Pasadena, a quaint city, just north of downtown Los Angeles, where the Rose Bowl Football Game and Tournament of Roses Parade are held each New Year's Day. Calvin stays diligent in prayer as he walks Historic Route 66, inching ever closer to Santa Monica State Park where he will arrive at the end of this week. It takes continued intention and purpose to stay focused now that the finish line is in sight. Images of home and our loved ones grow brighter each day as we count down to our homecoming date. In the meantime, we look forward to connecting with our friends Don and Net Lamb, who are planning to arrive in Los Angeles on Friday. It will be refreshing to see some familiar faces from home. Saturday we hope to visit the famous Griffith Park, adjacent to the familiar Hollywood sign and home to the much talked about Griffith Observatory and Los Angeles Zoo. Sunday, which marks the official end of the National Cross Walk 2014, we will attend Harvest Rock Church here in Pasadena. Monday we will be presenting the California staff to leaders of Harvest Rock Church and the greater Los Angeles region.

Please continue to pray for us as we finish the prayer walk and finalize preparations to begin the long journey across the country on our way home. No doubt the drive home will involve lots of reflection, reliving much of the past six months and preparing for the next season of life that awaits us in Lancaster, Pennsylvania. We have left a part of our hearts in each area where we sowed seeds of love and faith over the past five and one-half months, and are grateful for each person we met and the churches we connected with. You have all been such an important part of this journey. We are eternally grateful for your partnership and love. . . .

We drove up into the beautiful San Bernardino Mountains to Silverwood Lake. What a gorgeous oasis from the hustle and bustle in the valley.

As Calvin walked through California towards our final destination, the San Bernardino Mountains stayed on his right. We never got enough of these majestic mountains.

We spent Sunday morning at San Bernardino Community Church where the greater Los Angeles Teen Challenge Choir shared in song and testimonies.

Calvin and I outside the San Bernardino Community Church.

The Journey's End
July 26, 2014

On Thursday, July 17 at 12:22 p.m., Calvin planted his feet on the rustic sands of Santa Monica State Beach. At 12:44, his feet hit the cold waters of the Pacific Ocean. Relief, gratitude, and overwhelming feelings of amazement at what we had experienced over the past year to get to this place flooded over us. God has been so faithful to us as we literally "walked" through the tedious season of preparation, getting sponsors, trip planning, packing for the trip and each unique week of actually traveling across the nation, step by step, day by day.

Our good friends, Don and Net Lamb, traveled to the west coast to ensure we finished our journey alongside familiar faces. Friday, Calvin traveled back into Santa Monica State Beach with them to spend some time praying and proclaiming God's promises. Our day on Saturday was filled with sightseeing. We visited the Los Angeles Zoo and then trekked up to the Observatory at the top of Griffith Park where we had a fantastic view of the whole Los Angeles Metro area. Sunday we were blessed by hearing the Consulate General of Israel to Los Angeles, David Siegel, at Harvest Rock Church in Pasadena. He shared about Israel's conflict with radical elements in Gaza and Israel's struggle for survival during the past several weeks.

Monday night was the culmination of the National Cross Walk 2014. The leadership of Harvest Rock Church received us and graciously gave us some time during the School of Supernatural Ministry's service. We presented the California shepherd's staff to Harvest Rock Church. We also handed over fifteen letters, which had been written by strategic leaders from the East Coast, pronouncing blessing to the church and the West Coast region. While we were praying over the letters, a pastor in the audience saw a vision of water gushing up and out of the letters. This helped seal in our hearts the significance of the letters. Calvin is praying that they will release blessing and encouragement to the churches on the West Coast. We connected with our good friend, Brandon Hess, whose home church back east is Christ Community Church in Camp Hill, Pennsylvania. He and his wife, Tara, are part of Harvest Rock Church, where Brandon serves at the school as well as on the worship team. We were also privileged to hand deliver a shepherd's staff to Christeena Kale. The School of Supernatural Ministry presented her with the staff as a way to honor her leadership position at the school. God used Christeena to give us significant confirmation concerning the date and time of Calvin's arrival at Santa Monica Beach and the waters of the Pacific.

Now, as we drive thousands of miles back across the country, we are reliving dozens of adventures and reminiscing about the people we met and connected with. How can we affectively convey all that God did in us and through us over this past six months? How do we move into the next season of our lives with the same excitement and dedication? God's grace is the same for the mundane and ordinary stuff of life as it is for the sensational—perhaps even more so, since the uniqueness of our daily lives is often lost in the midst of monotony.

As most of you know, Calvin has been prayer walking for more than thirty years, and much of what he learned throughout that time, he was able to apply to our cross-country prayer walk. God is already beginning to birth vision in Calvin's heart for future walks.

We desire your continuing prayers for us as we transition back into work, relationships, and church life. Calvin will be returning to construction work, and I will be resuming my massage work as well as launching my health coaching business. God used your prayers and support to sustain us many times throughout the past year. We know God will reward your faithfulness with abundant blessings in every area of your lives.

Calvin walked straight through downtown Los Angeles on Santa Monica Boulevard.

Our final destination- Santa Monica Beach, California.

The Pacific Ocean has such a rugged beauty.

Calvin finally arrived at Santa Monica Beach!

Calvin mixed the sands from the East Coast with the sands of the West Coast.

How could Calvin not worship God for bringing us safely to our journey's end?

The infamous Los Angeles traffic.

Calvin and I took some time off to enjoy the creatures at the Los Angeles Zoo. The chimps are always one of our favorites at the zoo.

Zebra at the Los Angeles Zoo.

We drove back through downtown Los Angeles after our day of celebrating our arrival at the Pacific Ocean.

Don and Net Lamb flew out to Los Angeles to join us at the end of our journey.

These vibrantly-colored flamingos were a sight for sore eyes which had endured many weeks of drab desert colors.

The view of Los Angeles from the top of the Observatory, the highest point in Los Angeles.

The famous Hollywood sign greeted us during our visit to the Observatory.

Beautiful Pasadena City Hall.

Presenting fifteen letters from leaders on the East Coast to Harvest Rock Church and the believers on the West Coast.

We presented the California shepherd's staff to the leadership at Harvest Rock Church.

A special shepherd's staff was presented by the staff at the Supernatural School of Ministry to Christeena Kale who serves on the leadership team.

On our drive home, Calvin captured a beautiful display of God's glory in this Arizona sunset.

Our dear friends, the Bairds, showered us with their love and hospitality when we stayed with them twice throughout our cross country trip.

Our good friends, the Seibels, welcomed us to Colorado on our way back home to Pennsylvania.

It seems our car was just as full on the way home as it was when we started our trip back on January 31.

Home sweet home!

Getting a little help from Rosie with the huge chore of unpacking.

Together again with our daughter Sheila and two of our granddaughters, Abbi and Emma.

Reunion! Our daughter Alicia and her four children (from left to right) Dominic, Cassie, Brianna and Alexis.

AFTERWORD

Beyond the Veil

She slipped a piece of scrap paper into my hand as I stood and chatted with another woman after the service. Later when I opened it, the words leaped off the piece of crumbled paper, "You are a godly example of true submission, grabbing hold of the vision and supporting the call as ONE."

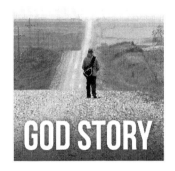

I closed the note and squeezed it hard, trying to squeeze out the accusations of the enemy. Submission . . . submission . . . a word that came off my tongue grudgingly and without heartfelt belief. How many times had I agreed to my husband's ideas in the past, but with skepticism and unbelief?

That incident happened more than a year ago. Since then, our amazing cross-country prayer walk as a husband and wife team runs long laps around my brain, reminders of our adventures still fresh in my thinking. Casual conversations and fleeting pictures still fill our lives and minds as my husband and I continue to learn from and relive many of the intimate experiences we had on our national cross walk. Did I truly "grab hold of the vision?" Did I whole-heartedly "embrace the call as one with my husband?"

So many days were filled with the pain of loneliness, the suffocation of isolation. Navigating strange cities and walking lonely, cold streets, fear trying to twist its way into my soul, keeping me from reaching out to those whose needs screamed out all around me. I am a survivor, and again I was surviving. But was that God's plan for me during the six-month assignment? Yes, *my* assignment—from the Lord, to me, for that season. In the same way that I had completed my assignment to homeschool and to raise our five children had I also completed this God-ordained assignment, given by my Heavenly Father? Had He trusted that I would complete it faithfully and with joy?

The stark reality of my situation had hit me square in the face, day after day, week after week. There, on the road, I was stripped of all that was familiar; all that I leaned on. The people that filled my life with joy and purpose were living far from the sound of my voice and the warmth of my hugs. Was I complete, whole without all those peripheral pieces of my life? How could I know true contentment without all the "stuff" of life that fed my soul and caressed my fragile ego? The process of refining, of burning away the unnecessary—the faux part of myself—had waged on and on, often bringing me to the point of emptiness and numbness of soul. While my husband chirped through each day, reveling in his new-found freedom, I on the other hand had resented his lack of compassion towards my inward struggles. Mine was a victory only God could bring, as He waged war on my behalf and wrote His unalterable truths upon my heart. My relationship with the God of the Universe, not my fickle circumstances, was my anchor, my strong tower. In the same way that He had sustained me, taught me, carried me through many difficult years, He empowered me to thrive, not just survive, during this season of sacrifice and surrender. But it was a process—one I needed to yield to minute by minute, hour by hour.

Each day I had tried to make a small dent into the steely walls of the world around me: Eking out a smile on the face of the woman who day after day cleaned up after the oblivious guests at the hotels. Thanking the grocery store cashier, as she absent-mindedly passed my purchases down the line, and letting her know how beautiful her town was. Letting the waitress know I was glad she could finally go home in an hour and thanking her for the infectious smile she still wore after a long ten-hour shift. Planting seeds, making a difference—all part of my assignment.

There were days I still missed so much—my family, my home and my pets, of knowing where I belonged. During our journey, Calvin and I lived in forty-four different hotels in 108 days. Strangers living next door to our rooms passed me silently in the hallways. Calvin was so much better at meeting new people, at opening his heart to those he had just met. I had extensive emotional boundaries that kept me safe and secure behind their psycho-sounding barriers, which neither friend nor foe could easily penetrate. They had to earn my trust—I would reassure myself that this was the safest course of action. In the meantime, lonely souls traipsed by me each day, heads hung, not daring to make eye contact. The world was a lonely place, filled with starving people, just waiting for an act of humanity to break open their fragile cocoon of isolation.

As weeks turned into months, I reluctantly let down some of my guard, allowing God to transform my fear into courage, empowering me to seize each day, seeing my assignment not as a dreaded lot to be borne, but rather as an honor, a privilege. I could intentionally walk alongside my husband, whose tenacity and purpose of heart inspired me each morning. Watching him trudge out into the sub-freezing dawn each day, turning into the relentless wind and making tracks in the spirit as well as the freshly-fallen snow was truly inspirational. Bearing up under the arid, scorching heat, reaching out to the homeless, the forgotten souls of the city streets caused the angels to smile, I know. God hadn't called me to walk through the harsh elements, traversing the cold and heat of the land, but He had called me to walk through the wasteland of the loneliness of my heart, bracing myself against self-pity, wrestling the lies that threatened to overwhelm me. This was just a season, but it was my season, to embrace, to conquer, to grab hold of and finally to let go. . . .

The Ripple Effect
August 9, 2014

Some of you may be questioning why you are receiving another update when we are settled back at home base after the National Cross Walk 2014 has been completed. Just as a stone that is thrown across the water sends out infinite ripples that reach further and further, touching everything in its path, so the fruit of The National Cross Walk continues to affect our lives as well as the many lives we touched over the past year.

Pastor Jeff from San Bernardino called Calvin this week and shared with excitement how their drought-ridden area had received some gentle monsoon rains, a rare phenomenon. He wanted Calvin to know that his fervent prayers for rain were being answered. This week we received an encouraging email from a sister that we met at North Church in April.

Despite these encouraging reminders of the impact the walk had on others, we find ourselves again thrown onto the "hamster wheel" of life, meeting deadlines, fulfilling obligations, paying bills and renewing relationships. We believe there are still many who need to hear about the faithfulness of God throughout our long journey and we are beginning to receive invitations to share our experiences. We know that each person or group we share with has unique needs and we are praying that what and how we share will be "customized" for that specific group.

It is necessary for us to move forward into the next season, but we do not want to forget all that God has accomplished through the National Cross Walk. His plans and purposes will be realized, not just through us, but through His body here on the earth. As we look ahead to new adventures, one thing we are assured of—His will will be done, and His kingdom will come, here on earth as it is in heaven. The next adventure awaits . . . count us in!

About Calvin and Stephanie Greiner

Stephanie Greiner Stephanie has a vision to see the church walk in health and wholeness in every area of life. She passionately pursues this vision as a health coach, licensed massage therapist, writer and life-long learner. Stephanie, whose home is in Lancaster County, Pennsylvania, enjoys the beach, swimming, reading and spending time with her husband and her five adult children and their families, including eight wonderful grandchildren. Her constant companions are her Golden Retriever and two Siamese cats.

Calvin Greiner Calvin has been prayer walking for more than thirty years. Calvin has prayer walked locally, regionally and nationally. He networks with the spiritual leadership in each area and connects the body of Christ in the spiritual, governmental and marketplace arenas. He and his wife, Stephanie, have recently completed a cross-country prayer walk from the East Coast to the Pacific Ocean.

Author Contact

For more information or for additional copies of this book, contact:

Calvin and Stephanie Greiner
The Ministry Center
PO Box 62
Manheim, PA 17545
Telephone: 717-799-8192
csgreiner@dejazzd.com
nationalcrosswalk.com